THE BUSINESS

Compiled and edited by
PAUL PRITCHARD

© Copyright 1992
ISBN 0 9520626 0 7

*Dedicated to the memory of
James Brown OBE
with gratitude and affection*

CONTENTS

YOUR FIRST PROFESSIONAL SYMPHONIC DATE
JEFFREY BRYANT
—— 1 ——

OPERA AND BALLET
JULIAN BAKER
—— 19 ——

THE HORN IN THE STUDIO
JOHN PIGNEGUY
—— 39 ——

SOLO PERFORMANCE AND CHAMBER MUSIC
FRANK LLOYD
—— 55 ——

GENERAL FREELANCE WORK
PAUL PRITCHARD
—— 87 ——

FOREWORD

I was very pleased when my friend Jeffrey Bryant asked me to write a few sentences for the forthcoming book entitled 'The Business'. However, a couple of instant confessions are due: my technical knowledge of the French Horn, how it is put together, how the various crooks came into being, and how historians view it, is lamentably small. Another admission: I don't play the Horn. What I really mean is that I cannot produce any kind of sound on it, of any persuasion. Most people, when attempting to wrest some sort of noise out of a Horn, manage to finally produce a rude sort of bleat, but I am incapable even of that.

But I genuinely love the sound of the instrument. I love it in the orchestra, and in chamber music, and as a solo instrument. From the elegance of Mozart to the extravagance of Strauss, the presence of the Horn fills me with pleasure. I have had the good luck to conduct many of the British orchestras. One of the undeniable strengths in these orchestras is the excellence of the English horn players. This is not simply an opinion, but an accepted fact, known throughout the international music world. Horn players, probably due to the fact that they play the riskiest of all instruments, tend to be interesting, if slightly eccentric people, and I have had a great deal of fun in their company. This book is a fine introduction into their world, with all its problems and perks. It makes for fascinating reading. Just don't forget to transpose each word!

INTRODUCTION

This is a very special publication. It contains an enormous amount of invaluable information for <u>all</u> musicians. I enjoyed reading it and learned a lot from it. A copy should be on every musician's book-shelf.

Barry Tuckwell

Barry Tuckwell. AC OBE

The unique experience of outstanding London hornplayers can be found here in a nutshell; including the psychological insight into being a performer. I myself have learnt a lot from working with these musicians over many years. I highly recommend this book to any aspiring performer, on the horn or any other instrument.

Vladimir Ashkenazy

Vladimir Ashkenazy

EDITORS NOTE

Every year a large number of instrumentalists graduate from colleges and universities, with the intention of making a living from music. Many of these people have the technique and confidence to achieve their aim without much difficulty. Why then is it that so many fail to make the grade?

When you first work with a professional orchestra, one thing you learn very quickly, is that it is taken for granted you can play your instrument efficiently and well. At college or university, technical prowess alone may have been sufficient to ensure your success, but now you are going to find that there are many other things to be taken into consideration.

That is the starting point of this book. Each chapter contains a great deal of valuable first-hand experience, which will help you get to know what you can expect in the early days of your career. Amongst other things, this book tells you: How to get work; how to organise yourself; how to play well in every environment from the concert hall, to the studio and West End theatres; how to avoid making 'New boy' mistakes that can undermine your confidence and distract you from your goal, which is to perform to the best of your abilities.

As you read through the book, you will probably notice that sooner or later, the same points appear in each chapter. These points are the true essentials of successful instrumental playing, and are repeated to emphasise their importance. A teacher is sometimes, for one reason or another, simply not able to find the exact approach for each pupil, to ensure that he, or she, fully understands these essentials. You will find these 'golden rules' stated five times in five different ways, by players who are active at the very heart of professional music making. It is our hope that one of these ways; or perhaps a mixture of all of them, will be right for you.

Obviously, no book of this kind can be fully comprehensive; you will no doubt, find yourself in situations that we have not covered. To cope with these, you must develop the ability to 'think on your feet'. Even so, the information contained in this book, will help you deal with most of the problems that you will encounter.

Although this book is written by horn players, for horn players, it is in no way a tutor. Most of the information is relevant to all instrumentalists.

I would like to thank everybody who has been involved with the production of this book, not least the enthusiastic and helpful comments of those who were coerced into reading the book in its early stages. Finally, my special thanks to Sally Gribble for correcting our wayward grammar.

YOUR FIRST PROFESSIONAL SYMPHONIC DATE

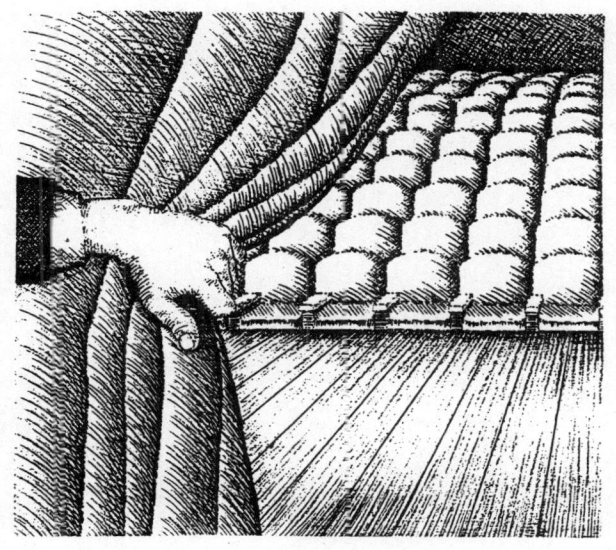

JEFFREY BRYANT

JEFFREY BRYANT

Jeffrey Bryant was born in Bristol in 1946. He took up the horn at the age of sixteen and soon joined the National Youth Orchestra. He then went on to the Royal Academy of Music to study with Ifor James. His first professional position, at the age of twenty, was with the BBC Midland Light Orchestra. Subsequently he became principal

horn of the Bournemouth Symphony Orchestra, followed in turn by principal positions with the London Philharmonic, and the London Symphony Orchestras. He has been principal horn of the Royal Philharmonic since 1975.

He has appeared regularly as a soloist with all of these orchestras and has recorded the Britten Serenade with the Royal Philharmonic conducted by Vladimir Ashkenazy.

He has been a professor at the Guildhall school of music since 1973.

So far you've done everything right (we hope). You've got a mouthpiece and a horn which suit you, you can play the whole range on the horn – high, middle, low and fortissimo to pianissimo, you can transpose and handstop, in fact you're probably a bit of a 'hot shot' at your college. One morning, very early, probably after a late night, you get a phone call from the fixer (personnel manager) of a full time professional orchestra. "Can you get to the Festival Hall/Barbican Hall by 10.00am, our first horn is ill?" In that one sentence there is a lot to be taken in. Perhaps I'd better explain.

First of all you'll be taken aback to be rung by the L.S.O., R.P.O/Berlin Phil. etc. Secondly, the fixer said that the first horn is ill. Does this mean that he wants you to play First horn? The answer to that is almost certainly "NO". After all he's never heard you play, so I don't think that he'd risk his job just to give you your big break. No, what he probably means is that he wants you to come in and 'bump-up', (assistant first) or possibly play third if the regular third horn steps up. In fact, he's probably a very desperate man because he's tried all his regular extras and none of them are available. He has to get a 'bum on a seat' and so he's taking a long shot by booking an untried student. If he doesn't get somebody, the horn section and the conductor will give him a very tough time.

That's how most people get started in the profession. Not because their reputation has gone before them necessarily, but to help out a fixer who is at the end of his tether. Your professor – who might in fact be the ailing first horn – has risked his reputation by giving the fixer your phone number.

The important thing is that your number remains on the extra list. If you are not free to do the date due to a commitment at college or a similarly binding engagement, your number will stay on his list for emergencies only. If you genuinely cannot do the date, the fixer won't hold it against you or 'black' you. It simply means that he has to make yet another phone call – probably to one of your fellow (rival?) students. That's why you must accept the date if at all possible. Don't risk being thrown out of your place of study though, for just one date it's not worth it; you'll get another chance.

Lets look on the bright side and assume that you can make it, even if a measure of bobbing and weaving is required. The next steps are very important. Make sure that you find out from the fixer, the exact times of the rehearsal(s) and concert(s) and the venue(s) including the address and phone number of the orchestra's office, just in case you have a problem, (illness, car breakdown etc) and last but not least, the dress to be worn, (tails, D.J. etc). While you are getting all this information, try to find out the repertoire that you will be playing and if possible, what part you are to play, so that you can mentally prepare yourself. A story (which may be apocryphal) concerns a student who was booked at short notice by a fixer who told him, in the time honoured fashion, that the rehearsal was 10 to 1 at the Royal Festival Hall. What he should have said of course, was that the rehearsal was from 10 <u>until</u> 1. The hapless student arrived in plenty of time for 12.50 but hopelessly late for ten o'clock.

MAKING THE MOST OF YOUR OPPORTUNITY

You have got a great opportunity and now you must make the most of it. To help you do this I'll try to pass on some tips that I have learned in my twenty five years as an orchestral musician. The first and probably most important piece of advice that I can give you, is perhaps the opposite of what you might expect; Try <u>not</u> to be noticed. You see, if you succeed in this, then you must be doing everything right. Whatever you do don't show off, remember that you are dealing with hard-bitten pros, and the only kind of impression that you are going to make is a negative one. They've seen too many band room soloists come and <u>go</u>. So take it easy and just get on with the job. When I say don't be noticed, it doesn't mean that you have to be standoffish – be polite and introduce yourself to the horn section, but don't feel that you have to make conversation. Remember that although it may be the most exciting day of your life, it's just another day's work for them. Also, they could probably do without having a new boy around, having to show him the ropes and hoping that he doesn't draw any unwanted attention to the section, so keep a low profile.

There are a lot of double standards in life and an orchestra is no exception. For example, the regular players may well talk, read magazines, (Dennis Brain always had a copy of 'Autocar' on his stand), or do the crossword. Don't fall into the trap of emulating them in this. It would be seen as a lack of respect. As a new boy you should be seen to be and should be, keen and attentive, and rightly so.

CHOICE OF INSTRUMENT

This is time when your choice of horn is very important. In my opinion you should be playing a middle of the road type instrument and certainly a double. It's no good turning up to play 4th horn on a B flat single horn, or even a B flat and high F even though all the notes are there. There are some first horns/horn sections who are very dogmatic about instruments. For instance they may all play Alexander horns and dislike Paxmans or vice versa. Don't be tempted to borrow a friend's horn if yours does not fit in. You are much better off with your own horn, after all, it's the only known quantity in a day full of surprises. Besides, if you do succeed in impressing them, (by not being noticed), then you may be asked back regularly. Maybe that would be the time to consider a change of equipment.

FITTING INTO THE SECTION

Perhaps it would be useful to enlarge on the notion of not being 'noticed'. I don't mean that you should not pull your weight, far from it. To go' 'unnoticed' you must fit in with the corporate section sound. If they play with their bells free, then you must too, if they play with their bells on their leg, then you follow suit.

Similarly, if the sound is bright, imitate it, if it's dark then you must try to make yours the same. Listen hard to sort out the intonation but don't talk about it. That can be misconstrued and taken as an insult. Musicians are a touchy lot, so don't make it obvious when you adjust the tuning slide. Don't look at your horn, ponder, and then push in or pull out, try to be a little more subtle. Sort out whether you are sharp or flat by adjusting your hand position, take your time and when you are sure, take out your tuning slide as if you were going to tip out the water, (even if you have a water key), and when you replace the slide, put it back in the new position. You may have to go through this rigmarole more than once, but take it from me it's well worth the trouble.

As a student, you most probably think that professionals play incredibly loudly; well they do. If you can match their volume, then fine, but don't force the sound or push your luck. My advice is that you should play one notch under their loud dynamics; that way you will get carried along with the overall volume. In my experience, many young inexperienced musicians don't act intelligently in this respect. They get caught up in the excitement, which is understandable, and try to play too loudly. This often results in 'putting it all over the ceiling' – not just once, but time after time. This is definitely not impressive, certainly not appreciated, and very 'noticeable'. Remember that the rest of the section have been playing for years, have bags of experience and enormous strength and stamina. Just hold back a fraction and you'll find that you will be much more accurate.

DYNAMICS AND ENTRIES

In addition to playing extremely loudly, you will discover that 'ppp' really is just that – incredibly quiet. My advice here is that you should have sorted out this aspect of your playing during your years of studying and practising. Loud playing can be learned on the job, quiet playing cannot. From the outset of your professional career, you must be able to play 'pp' entries, (high middle and low register), with 99% security. Likewise, you must be able to hold a 'pp' long note on your own, solo, in any register, without hesitation and in tune. I can't emphasise this enough, your whole career will depend on this. One piece of advice that I can give you is never, never be the first in on a 'pp' entry. Just wait an extra millisecond – for two reasons: firstly it's going to sound much more together, and secondly, if you do fluff the note, it will be far less obvious. The 'covering fire', so to speak, of the other players might even render your fluff inaudible.

When you sit in the orchestra, don't be a 'lighthouse'. 'Lighthouse' is jargon for anyone who is always looking around. Try not to turn around and look at anyone, keep your head forward, – especially if there are any mistakes being made by other players. This is an important part of orchestral etiquette and musicians are very hot on it. You will certainly be tempted to 'lighthouse for', after all, everything will be new and fascinating, but don't do it. However, you should observe and take in as much as possible. This can be done by moving your head only a fraction, and your eyes a lot. It sounds strange, but it's amazing what you can see in this unobtrusive way.

BUMPING UP

If you are bumping up, (playing assistant first), there are several important things to remember if you want to be invited back. You are there for the sole purpose of making the first horn's job easier, thereby enabling him to play at his or her best. You are not being paid to have a good blow through a piece, although you will have to work hard. I'll try to explain how to succeed as a bumper. Firstly and most importantly, count the bars rest and follow the music being played, even if you are not required to play a single note of the passage or movement. You must always know where you are and what the transposition is, so that should the first horn get lost, you can give him the information that he needs, or even more importantly, stop him from coming in early. Take it from me, you can score millions of points this way. If in the middle of a passage the first horn turns to you, and asks, panic-struck, "Where are we?" Stay calm, KEEP COUNTING, nod, and tell him just as soon as possible. You might have to play a couple of notes if there isn't time to communicate. Whatever you do, don't do what people have done to me in the past and say "Pardon?" In fact, don't say anything except the relevant bar number or transposition, otherwise you will both be lost, and this would NOT BE GOOD.

Turning the pages is also the bumper's responsibility. Sounds easy doesn't it? but not so. I have been thrown countless times by careless page turning, non page turning and even by turning two pages at once. You must be certain that the first horn has clocked the number of remaining bars on the page before you turn. When you do turn, you must ensure that you don't obscure the bottom line, or the last few bars of music with your arm or hand. To avoid this you have to lean a long way across and turn the page either from the top, or from the bottom with your thumb or forefinger. Practise this, it is important. If you are prepared to take notice of all these things, then you will be well on your way to being a successful bumper, a highly rewarding and much appreciated job.

The passages to be bumped are frequently marked in the part by the first horn. If they are not, you should establish with the first horn exactly what they require you to play. Sometimes this is not possible, as some players are very vague, or do not wish to be tied down by rigid markings. This makes life a little difficult for the bumper, but a good 'rule of thumb' under the circumstances is to play too little, rather than too much. The theory behind this is that it is much easier to get someone to play by gesturing (such as leaning forward in the chair), than it is to stop them playing. If you are both playing together, any gesture might look like an indication to carry on playing. It is also very irritating to have someone playing along with you in your favourite passage from a particular work. If the principal indicates that they want some unscheduled bumping, don't panic and rush in, you will probably mess up the entry if you do. You should take as much time as is necessary to ensure a clean articulation.

While on this subject, most bumper mistakes are due to a lack of commitment, caused by an uncertainty whether to play or not. As a bumper you must plan ahead and decide which note you intend to come in on and be 100% positive about it, even a little assertive.

If you are required to take over in a long, tiring, quiet passage, you are much more likely to fluff the entry, or come in with a clumsy articulation if you enter at the beginning of a note. It is far better to ease in on an offbeat for some obscure reason. For example, if you have a semibreve written, insert an imaginary quaver rest at the beginning of the bar or take over on the last quaver of the bar. Try it, it works!

PLAYING SECOND HORN

As I have never held the position of second horn, I am not equipped to give you specialist advice on that subject but I can tell you my personal likes, dislikes and opinions, which just might be helpful to you. First of all a special kind of personality is required. The second horn in a symphony orchestra has to work extremely hard, frequently in the least rewarding register of the instrument. For all their hard work, they get very little in the way of glory or even credit. In my experience, they are usually extremely accomplished players who, by some fluke of birth, have the ability but not the nerve, thick skin, arrogance, – call it what you will, to play 1st horn. It is essential that they should be a 'complete' player, as accuracy in the low, middle <u>and</u> high registers is essential. To refer to a 2nd horn as a low player is a misnomer. True, one's greatest strengths should be in the middle and low register, but <u>not</u> at the total expense of the high register. A second horn's high register should be <u>totally</u> secure, but not necessarily scintillating.

The articulation of a second player has to be exceptionally good as, unlike the first, he does not decide the precise timing of an entry. He has to follow his principal – and by follow him, I don't mean come in after him but actually with him. This is the second special attribute which a really good no.2 needs. It's a mixture of sensitivity, musicality and sixth sense. This cocktail of qualities enables him to feel exactly when his partner is going to make an entry, change the emphasis of a phrase, crescendo or diminuendo and so on. It's rather like getting into someone else's skin (see 'Silence of the Lambs'!). I have had some marvellous experiences of second horns 'shadowing' me perfectly. So perfectly in fact, that they made me sound better than I really am. This should be the aim of every 2nd horn – to make two instruments sound like one. Referring back to the sixth sense, I worked for a time with a player who was so much 'in my skin' that he even knew when I was counting incorrectly! Amazing, and very useful.

INTONATION

Perhaps the most difficult aspect of playing second is intonation. You always have to tune to the 1st horn, even if you believe him to be way out of tune. This is difficult because it means that you will not be in tune with other instruments that are playing in unison or octaves with you. When you are put in this impossible situation, my advice is to use a light to heavy vibrato, depending on the severity of the problem. You will be amazed at how effective this can be. Never be dogmatic about intonation, always be sensitive and try to adjust to fluctuating pitch. Don't try to impose your pitch on a tricky passage by playing louder. Play quietly and try to merge into the overall sound. Talking of merging, don't ever be tempted to lead the high tutti passages from the second chair. In my experience this is never constructive and frequently disastrous! Box clever in these passages, let the 1st and 3rd set the pace. Concentrate instead on being accurate and in tune with a full sound. Playing second to an unfamiliar 1st horn is not at all easy; it takes time to build up a rapport and that 'sixth sense' we talked about. However, if you take note of the preceding advice and use your ears, you won't go too far wrong.

THE THIRD HORN

My view of the third horn position, is that it should be used as a stepping stone to being a first horn, and you therefore need a person who is ambitious, keen, talented and full of confidence. There is nothing wrong with making it clear that you wish to play first horn eventually, as long as you also make it clear that you are prepared to go to another orchestra to achieve your ambition. Your principal would take an extremely dim view of any attempt to depose him or her, and would no doubt resort to an arsenal of self-defence strategies, (dirty tricks), in order to defend themselves. Remember they will have years of experience to their credit, and more importantly, it is <u>their</u> job; and as everyone knows, possession is 9/10ths of the law! Far better to learn from their example, (maybe even a few of their dirty tricks), enjoy your music-making, learn the repertoire and get plenty of 'hands-on' experience both musically and politically.

In my opinion, this job is the most enjoyable in the section. You get enough solos to keep you on your toes and musically satisfied, together with plenty of exciting unison tunes to play. This is really your area of responsibility in the section; you have to provide weight during loud and/or high tuttis, so that the first horn can take it slightly easier, in order to be at his best for difficult solo passages. For instance, in a piece such as Strauss' 'Ein Heldenleben', the 1st horn must pace himself very carefully, so that he has the strength <u>and</u> sensitivity to play the extremely demanding solos that come at the end of the piece. The third horn does not have the same problem, and can support the principal by committing him/herself to every tutti, with the confidence of knowing that nothing need be kept in reserve.

THE TEMPERAMENT OF THE FOURTH HORN

The temperament required to be a good fourth horn is very similar to that of the second – in fact many of them have played second at some time in their career, and still take the opportunity to 'step up' to second when the occasion demands. The fourth horn should have the darkest sound in the section, in order that the bass notes of the horn 'choir' are full and round. The low register should be given more attention than that of the second horn. This will invariably mean that the high register suffers correspondingly. This must however, only be minimal, as although the 4th will venture into the higher registers far less frequently than the 2nd horn, (who has to cope with Mozart, Haydn and Bruckner etc) it should be secure, and perhaps more importantly, discreet. Discretion, for the experienced fourth horn, is in many cases the better part of valour.

On this topic, it is important not to show off and overplay the pedal notes, tempting as that might be. Audiences do not come to concerts to hear the fourth horn demonstrating his virtuosity in the low register – not twice anyway! Finally, and this is <u>not</u> a negative point, knowing what to leave out is the key to a long and successful career in the fourth horn chair.

THE QUALITIES NECESSARY TO PLAY FIRST HORN

Before I talk about the qualities required to be a successful first horn, I think that it is important to remember that although <u>every</u> orchestral player needs the same attributes, in the case of the principal horn, he must posses these qualities to a greater degree. He must be able to play over the full range of the horn, both in terms of register, and dynamics. My opinion is that pianissimo, is more important than fortissimo – in fact it is essential to excel in 'pp', even if it means that one's fortissimo is merely adequate. The reverse situation is a recipe for disaster in the long term. No–one in my experience has ever been sacked for not being able to play loudly enough, although I have seen the demise of many a player who could not control 'pp' entries and passages. Of course ones own goal is to excel in all dynamics however extreme; and being able to switch from one to the other while still retaining complete control, is one of the toughest technical challenges that we have to face.

It should go without saying that the first horn's high register should be rather special, with an ability to make difficult, high passages sound easy and unstrained. Again, this ability does not excuse a poor middle or lower register. <u>Every</u> note must be there, the repertoire demands it. For example: from top 'B' to pedal 'E' in Shostakovitchs' fifth symphony, from top 'C' to pedal 'C' in Strauss' 'Till Eulenspiegel', top 'A' to pedal B flat in Mussourgskys' 'Pictures from an exhibition' and top 'C' to pedal B flat in Strauss' 'Ein Heldenleben'. The repertoire is full of such demanding pieces as these, so take note, the first horn is not just a high player.

Here is a list of attributes which in my opinion are essential if you are to become – and more importantly – to remain, a first horn: determination, belief in oneself, strong constitution, strong nerve, flexibility, fantastic powers of concentration, mental toughness, sensitivity, opportunism, resilience, political awareness, leadership, single-mindedness, sense of humour, independence, team spirit, large ego and a measure of arrogance. You will notice that some of the qualities appear to be contradictory, well, that goes some way towards explaining why first horns are not the most straightforward people that you are likely to meet; indeed these internal personality clashes are what makes them rather special. It is important to react to pressure in a positive way, and – this has been made clear to me many times – top players actually perform at their very best when the pressure is greatest. Despite this, they must still be able to play in a way that allows the audience, and their colleagues to relax and enjoy their performance. Finally, they must have something musically to say, and be able to project their personality into the music. Strong musical views are essential, but they can cause problems. One's firmly held musical views can frequently be in opposition of those of the conductor. Under these circumstances you really have no choice but to play it his way. You might win an occasional battle with a 'maestro', but you will never win the war! This is difficult to accept, particularly for younger players. When, for example, a young and inexperienced conductor is kind enough to 'teach' you a solo which you have probably played many times for truly great Maestros, it is hard to take, but take it you must. It's too hard going to try and change their minds, and in any case, you'll get a chance to play it your way some other time.

Finally, for your own sanity remember this: work incredibly hard, care so much, try so hard, yet, if things go wrong, be able to laugh it off. The world won't end because of your cracked note!

GENERAL ADVICE

Having given you specific advice on how to approach each position in the section, I want to take you now through a few more general tips.

If you warm up, (which I sincerely hope that you do), don't be overtly flashy, even if your normal warm-up is, shall we say, impressive. Do it at home if you can, or at least be very discreet – stick a mute in, or find a back stage room or corridor. Once people get to know you, it's OK to just play away – unless of course the harpist is tuning. Then you will have to go elsewhere, or wait until he/she has finished. Given that you have the time, it makes good sense to prepare the repertoire, and to establish which part you will be required to play.

Now a few 'social tips'. As a youngster you will be expected to run for the teas at the break. If you are bumping, the first horn may even send you out just before the break is due to make sure that you are at the front of the queue. Even third place in the queue can mean a long wait for refreshments, especially if you are behind a bass player buying eight teas, or a 'cellist' providing for the fourteen members of his section. So, without resorting to physical violence, make sure that you achieve what you were sent to do. Your efforts will be much appreciated; for a hard working musician, the break is one of the highlights of the rehearsal! Don't however emulate the first-timer, who, after being sent out early to get the teas, brought them back into the rehearsal hall on a tray while work was still in progress! Amusing, but definitely NOT the way to go unnoticed.

If you are invited to go to the pub/winebar, do go but avoid alcohol. Many Pro's. drink a lot, but it's not a good idea; in fact I'd go so far as to say that it's a very bad idea. Do yourself a favour and stick to mineral water, or something else non-alcoholic. This dictum does not apply to after the show, a few beers will go down a treat and will help you to unwind. It really is not necessary to be one of the boys (especially if you're a girl!), to get started or get on in the music business. Just be your own man/woman and be polite and pleasant. If you can play, you should have no trouble succeeding.

PREPARING FOR THE CONCERT

To get back to the music, when the rehearsal is over, take the music home with you, having first asked permission, and with your horn in your hand go through everything, fingering but not playing any of it. This will get it into your head without knocking out your lip. Make sure that you arrive in plenty of time for the concert. Give yourself at least fifteen minutes to prepare both your lip and your mind. Find somewhere quiet and 'programme' yourself. The opening of the concert will be a big shock; gone will be the 'laid back' attitude of the rehearsal, and in its place will be an electric atmosphere, intense concentration and total commitment. This is the SHOW, everybody really means business. To cope with the radical change of atmosphere, I prepare myself by creating a mental picture of myself in concert dress performing successfully in front of an audience. With particularly difficult concerts I start this 'brainwashing' process weeks before the event, but it can work for less pressured concerts in a shorter space of time. As little as an hour can be enough, this may sound a little odd but it definitely helps me get over my nerves.

Here are a few final suggestions to help you make a successful debut:

> When someone tells you something, never say "I know" even if you do. Simply say 'thank you'.
>
> Don't fidget, empty water noisily or adjust your music stand in a concert.
>
> Should anyone be kind enough to praise you, accept gracefully – it's insulting if you don't.
>
> Avoid talking about politics, religion, intonation and the opposite sex in orchestras, all are highly emotive subjects.
>
> Always have a pencil and rubber handy, preferably clipped to your horn.

After reading this far, you may feel that getting started in the music profession is too daunting. If that is the case, just follow this last piece of advice; be enthusiastic and enjoy your music making. If you really love music, love playing the horn and can play it well, you'll make it. Incidentally, I have made all the mistakes in this book – and more – and I'm still playing and <u>enjoying</u> it So you see, your career definitely will not depend on getting everything right according to all the things that I have mentioned – but it just might help if you do.

USEFUL POINTS

Ensure that you have all the relevant information from the 'fixer' e.g. venue, time, dress, part to be played, repertoire, phone number of venue. <u>Repeat back to fixer.</u>
Try not to be 'noticed'. Keep a low profile.
Use a 'middle of the road' horn and mouthpiece combination.
Always listen and blend.
Adjust tuning SUBTLY.
Don't read magazines/books/papers.
Perfect your 'pp' NOW.
Never be first in on an entry.
Always count, even if there are cues in the part.
Always warm up.
Avoid alcohol.
Always have a pencil and rubber.
Arrive early and programme your mind.
Bump too little rather than too much.

COMMON MISTAKES

Double booking.
Wrong time, venue or dress.
Late arrival.
Flashy 'band room' playing.
Making too much conversation e.g. telling your life story or the contents of your diary.
Borrowing a horn just to fit in.
'Lighthousing'.
Overblowing.
Switching off when not required bumping-up.
Excessive consumption of alcohol.
Over-bumping.
Fluffing entries through not planning your bumping and rushing in.
Fighting conductors.
2nd/4th being heroes in high tutti passages.
Over specialisation in high or low register.

OPERA & BALLET

JULIAN BAKER

JULIAN BAKER

The son of an organist and a music teacher, Julian Baker received his first musical education as a pupil at Lichfield Cathedral School. Here he was taught the horn by Frank Downes. After completing his studies at the Royal College of Music, at the age of twenty, he was appointed to the position of principal horn with the Halle Orchestra, by Sir John Barbirolli.

He remained in Manchester for seven years before joining the B.B.C. Symphony Orchestra under Pierre Boulez. Seven years later he left to take up his present post with the orchestra of the Royal Opera House Covent Garden.

In 1974 he became a professor at the Royal College of Music, where he has since had the pleasure of teaching students from all over the world.

INTRODUCTION

Playing in an Opera or Ballet orchestra has many built-in rewards in terms of personal satisfaction and achievement. In common with most other jobs, there are also problems and pitfalls which, although sometimes substantial, can with care, be avoided as you go along. The object of this chapter is to give you a picture of the dangers, as well as the pleasures involved in this kind of job. My own job with the Royal Opera House means that I am part of a large group of people, all of whom are striving in their own different ways, to put together a production of the highest possible standard and maintain that standard throughout a run of performances. The Royal Opera House provides a theatre for both Ballet and Opera, and consequently the repertoire for the orchestra covers an enormous range of all kinds of music from Baroque to contemporary.

THE JOB ITSELF

As a member of an Opera House orchestra, you will find yourself performing under conditions that you have never encountered before. They can be overcrowded and – especially on tour – downright primitive. This leads to all kinds of difficulties, for instance hearing yourself and others properly, and being aware of the general balance within the pit. There are even times when it is impossible to hear whether other instruments are playing or not. Notes that you may have thought were solo, are suddenly found to be merely part of a 'PP' chord being played by the wind or strings. It is perhaps the acoustical problems encountered when performing in a pit, that most highlight the contrast between this job and that of a symphonic player.

It is up to you to organise your comfort as best you can without upsetting your neighbour. The individually lighted music stands are unwieldy but generally adequate, although the optimum position for your own music stand may leave your neighbour unsighted. Working under these conditions, it is always worth compromising in order to keep the peace. Surprisingly in view of the proximity of one player to another, few accidents occur; no doubt due to the extra care that each player takes to protect his or her own instrument.

TUNING

Tuning in the pit has its own special problems. While of course one must be in tune with the principal and other members of the section, it is worthwhile keeping your ears open for general intonation in the pit, by focusing your attention on a larger section of the orchestra preferably not too close to your own. The 'cellos', for example play a similar range to the horn and are good indicators of pitch. The pitch of all orchestral instruments varies according to the temperature and humidity, which can reach uncomfortable extremes. Under these conditions, brass instruments will naturally rise in pitch, woodwind also; however the strings will tend to go the other way. In anticipation of this they sometimes compensate by adjusting the tension of the strings, giving a brighter edge to the sound. Over a long opera or ballet, this can sometimes result in different blocks of intonation dispersed throughout the orchestra. This can then affect the tuning within each section, as each player tries to cope with the problem in his or her own way.

Although this is a difficult situation, with a little humility and an awareness of the principles of tuning, it can be overcome.

FOLLOW YOUR INSTINCTS

This is also true of balance and ensemble. Certain passages, not obviously solos, need to be brought out in the overall texture of the piece. Thickly orchestrated music has often to be played at well under the specified dynamics (which are always relative anyway), but on the other hand, one must not be afraid to bring out a note marked piano, or a similarly marked phrase, if your instinct tells you to do so. Always remember that it is easier to reduce from a firm, confident dynamic, than from one which is already uncomfortably quiet. Some conductors while retaining overall control of the dynamics of the piece, will automatically expect you to adjust within the ensemble. This is why if you can show in an audition that you have this extra and creative imagination, it will mark you down as a likely candidate for the job. This ability will keep the conductor happy, and that is of course, the prime consideration at all times!

CONDUCTORS

To quote from Farquarson Cousins marvellous book 'On playing the Horn', there was the 'girl player who, when complaining that she was suffering from overwork, remarked that she "simply must get away from music". Her desk partner dryly advised her to marry a conductor.' Joking apart, some conductors, while not necessarily being 'good' conductors, have keener ears than most. It is quite usual for these maestros to send notes to players after each performance, concerning their intonation or ensemble. The significance of this is that unlike a single orchestral performance, where it is possible to play how you are instructed to in rehearsal but 'do it your way' in the show; with multiple performances you will have to do as you are told most of the time. I must add here that because of the problems that exist in the pit, it is vital that everyone plays 'on' the beat, so that there is at least a chance of unanimity in respect of ensemble.

DYNAMICS

It is often tempting to play louder than the singers on stage can cope with, and then try to justify your dynamics to yourself because they are written in the part. In view of the fact that the combination of modern instruments and exposed pits make the sound and balance very unlike that which was originally envisaged by the composer, this is a very shaky argument. This applies equally well to Haydn and Mozart as it does to Richard Strauss. We all know how exciting some passages are played forcefully, but the projection of a clear sound is an ideal for which one should strive constantly in a theatre pit, and only on rare occasions will the conductor give you a free rein to play as you like. After a while, you will get to know the individual approach of each conductor to these and other stylistic matters. They all have their idiosyncrasies, and while, if they do address you in rehearsal, it is sometimes tempting to be 'funny' rather than humorous with them, this will nearly always be counter-productive. After all, you can always give vent to your feelings about them after the rehearsal!

A sense of humour is essential during the long and frequently tedious rehearsals, (which all too often seem to have been called for the benefit of everyone except the orchestra), but politeness, often in the face of provocation, is always appreciated. Tempers can become frayed all too easily in the pit, especially towards the end of the season; we have all learned this the hard way.

HOW TO COPE WITH THE JOB

After your initial trial period, (which is initially usual 3 months and sometimes a further nine), once you have established yourself in the section, it is important to keep your playing up to scratch. One of the difficulties in doing this stems from the number of rehearsals that are often necessary, particularly in the cases of an opera or ballet that has not been performed for some years. It does not usually take long to become familiar with your own part, but there will be rehearsals for each act with the orchestra alone, followed – in the case of opera – by maybe two 'sitzproben' with the principals, then rehearsals (for each act), involving the whole cast on-stage, and finally a stopping run-through and a dress rehearsal. All this takes place before a run of anything from six to fifteen performances! Companies such as Glyndebourne and touring operas may have considerably more over the entire season.

You can understand that while the music might be difficult (or not) to play, and each performance quite tiring, you will not have the variety within the repertoire to keep your playing at a high standard without the stimulus of extra practice. Regular exercises and long notes will help you avoid the slow but steady decline into mediocrity, out of which it is difficult to climb. Long notes are especially rewarding, as they help you to maintain a good quality sound. As it is often difficult to monitor exactly what is emerging from one's bell in a pit, they will help to ensure that this, surely one of the most treasured parts of one's playing, does not deteriorate as well. It must become a matter of pride with you to learn the part as quickly as possible and maintain your initial high standard throughout the run.

It is also therapeutic, perhaps even necessary, to develop a hobby outside music that will help keep your interest in the job. Performances often finish late, and there are then rehearsals to be attended the following morning for a different work. You must try to feel sufficiently rested to be able to switch readily from one style of music to another. Six hours of Wagner, followed by Mozart twelve hours later, is not an easy transition. You will learn to pace yourself not only during the day, but during the evening performance when, usually without the benefit of an assistant principal, one's lip and powers of sustained concentration, (in Wagner, for example), are put to the ultimate test. It is useful to be able to rest for an hour of so during the day, especially between the rehearsal of one piece and the performance of another. Be careful not to overdo things during a rehearsal however good your lip feels, – it can take the edge off your performance that evening. Matinees followed by an evening show pose a particular problem, but it is odd (and fortunate), how even a short rest will sometimes give you a second wind for the evening.

STAGE BANDS

A stage band can involve anything from just one solo note, or Siegfried's horn call, right up to a large group of players, (for example those used in Verdi's operas.) This can be considered as a perk of the job, as you are often going to finish work quite early on in the evening – 'Rigoletto' is a wonderful example. On the other hand you might find yourself free for most of the evening, playing only at the beginning and the end of the performance. In Meterbeers 'LES HUGUENOTS' for example, the stage band is not called until 1/4 hour before the end of the opera! This could be a little dangerous if one is socially inclined! Always allow yourself plenty of time to get back to work, so that you are not too rushed. Warm up again if necessary. It has been known for performances to run a little ahead of the official timings – there are few situations more embarrassing than when the atmospheric horn call, that should be emanating from the depths of some theatrical forest – as in the third act of Verdis' 'Falstaff', is replaced by an eloquent, though from the audiences' point of view baffling silence. I once arrived to play the final brief offstage phrase in 'Gotterdammerung' with perhaps only three seconds to spare. Luckily, it was a good if somewhat breathless performance, but not until the next day did I discover that due to the arctic draught that my instrument had been lying in, I had sounded nearly a semitone flat! This prompts me to say two things: never rely on someone not involved intimately with the performance to tell you the timings of your calls, and always have the main and the valve slides pushed well in. Notwithstanding the cold, the distance between you and the audience will tend to make the pitch sound flat. It helps to ask a friend in the pit to check your pitch for you in rehearsals.

THE WAGNER TUBA

While this can be a marvellously rewarding instrument to play, it can also be so treacherous that you might feel embarrassed to take the extra fee that you are offered for playing it! The tuning of these instruments is notoriously difficult to cope with; the lower notes of the 'F' tuba presenting on some instruments a particular challenge, especially where articulation is concerned. Having said that, the 'Alexander' tubas such as the ones we use at Covent Garden are highly sophisticated, and repay all your efforts to play them well. Although you can buy double tubas in B flat and 'F', it is more usual to have a section of two B flat tenor (with the open harmonics of the 'F' put through a fourth valve) and two 'F' bass tubas with a similar valve putting the instrument down (again only by the open harmonics) to 'C'. With the combination of fingerings that are available, you can usually find suitable (if unconventional) fingerings to cover all eventualities. It may also be necessary in the cause of good intonation, to move the main turning slide between phrases.

The tubas must be practised well in advance of the first rehearsal, not least to familiarise yourself with the instrument, but also to free any valves which may have welded themselves to their casings during the sometimes lengthy intervals in between usage. You might find yourself involved in a 'tubas only' sectional rehearsal with the conductor, often before the first full rehearsal. Be warned that he will expect you to be totally familiar with the instrument. Therefore it is essential that you are already <u>playing</u> the part rather than 'wrestling' with it. Good intonation is certainly important but the production of a good sound is equally necessary. These instruments were intended by Wagner to bridge the gap between the horns and the large orchestral tuba, and to provide a contrast with, as well as a complement to the trumpets and trombones. Their present form stems from instruments developed over a twenty year period in time for the first complete performance of the Ring cycle in 1876.

To produce the intended mellow sound, the tubas must be played firmly, maximising the larger bore of the instrument by greater breath and embouchure control. Generally the tubas are employed for melodic passages in conjunction with the bass tuba and lower brass, rather than loud and forceful passages, and most effectively as a solo quartet (as in the Ring cycle). Richard Strauss writes some difficult parts for tubas – 'Elektra' for example – and these really <u>must</u> be looked at in advance. You will find that he writes in an uncompromisingly virtuosic way for them, just as he does for the horn and consequently makes greater demands on the player than any previous composer.

There are study books available for most of the Wagner tuba repertoire which, even without a tuba to hand, could profitably be examined to unravel some of the mysteries of tuba notation. Although the tuba parts are almost always originally written as a combination of Bb tenor and F bass, it is now common to find transposed parts all in F. It can initially be intimidating to see an edition of Siegfried, in which the 4th bass tuba seems to have a written high B in the treble clef, only to realise with no little relief that it should be played an octave lower.

The range of notes demanded from all four tuba parts is extensive. The tenor tuba is required to play up to top 'C' at the end of Rheingold, and to 'B' in Elektra and The Rite of Spring'. The bass tubas have to be very agile in Elektra too and horn players who are in the habit of playing extensively on the 'F' side of their own instrument, will find that the difficulties are more easily overcome. Sectional practice is vital, particularly before a performance, in order to achieve unanimity of pitch.

After a while you will find for yourself the most comfortable way of sitting and holding these awkward instruments, that will enable you to see both the music and the conductor. You must also make sure that you have enough room to rest the instruments while they are not being played. As there are often quite long gaps between passages, instrument stands should usually be provided. These will help you to pick up and put down the tuba in the shortest time possible. It is a good idea to have a separate mouthpiece for both the horn and the tuba, so that if the change over has to be really rapid, it can be done with the minimum of chaos in an overcrowded pit. I feel that I should put in a word about tuba mutes at this point – the most appropriate one that springs to mind is 'sabotage'! Very few tuba mutes seem to have any contribution to make to the proceedings other than a negative one, to the extent that they are often dispensed with altogether. (It is best to try this without asking the conductor.) However, a definitive design may be just around the corner – stranger things have happened – until then, the best of luck with them.

In spite of the difficulties that are involved, the satisfaction that can be gained from a good performance on these instruments will be ample recompense for all the extra effort.

FINANCIAL ASPECTS

A word about the financial aspects of the job. Most Opera and Ballet companies will have a yearly renewable contract with a negotiated minimum salary, which is for wind players a reasonable, if not excessive one. Sometimes there are also incentives for those who wish to stay in the orchestra and make their career in this field. However, due to the relative esteem in which the cultural well being of this nation is held, compared to that of other European countries, and until the time comes that adequate subsidies make artistic excellence affordable by all, and above compromise in the name of cutting costs, the incentives for making this your career will still seem poor in relation to other major European Opera houses.

There are increasingly available annuity schemes within orchestras, which contribute about half of the premiums attached to one's own private pension scheme, with a minimum total sum of about 10% of one's basic annual income from that source. There are also rewards from overtime worked, and extra sessions that can make a considerable difference to ones basic income, especially when it involves television, and of course commercial recordings and radio broadcasts. It is still possible to undertake a certain amount of freelance work outside the Opera house if one wishes. This is due to the fact that most of the pieces in the repertoire need fewer players than the total number on the payroll. A rota system is employed, but it can still be frustrating having to refuse an interesting engagement because it clashes with yet another rehearsal of the most boring piece in the repertoire. With a little advance planning however, and a little tact, there can be flexibility if one remains on good terms with the management.

All in all, it is a satisfying and stable way of earning a living, with a great number of exciting moments and an interesting environment in which to work. To get the best out of your time playing Opera or ballet, make sure that you keep practising, know when to keep quiet – musically and verbally –and above all, maintain and demonstrate your enthusiasm for this demanding but rewarding job.

THE AUDITION

It is worth telling you what to expect at an audition, as the mental preparation is very important in order that you are not intimidated by the circumstances. The first round of the audition will allow the candidates to show, in a short time, that they have talent, musicianship and personality. You will not get a second chance at this stage unless you impress the audition panel. This will consist –depending on the local conditions and rules – of some or all of the Horn section, some other principals, (probably wind players), the orchestral manager and possibly the conductor. This may seem a large number of people, but depending on availability of any of them on the day, may not usually add up to more than six or eight.

The audition will be overseen by either the principal horn, or, (if it is the principal position which has been advertised), the conductor, or possibly a well-known player from a different orchestra. Don't forget that while the horn section will have a good idea of who is likely to fit into the section both musically and socially, and may know you by reputation or as a freelance colleague and therefore as a friend, the other panel members have an equal say in determining the result. They will have a more dispassionate, and therefore clearer view of the proceedings – we, as horn players, know what can go wrong in various circumstances and why, but they on the other hand will only be in a position to judge what they hear on the day. Having said this, the whole panel will be fair and select the player most suitable for the vacant position. If you think that you have played well enough to deserve a trial with the orchestra but are not offered one, then the panel will have based their decision on matters of style and type of sound that you produce, rather than on any technical deficiency. Understanding this will encourage you to gain from the experience, analyse the situation, and enter for your next audition with full confidence.

PREPARATION

As a player, whether you are still at college, have recently left, are already established as a freelance player, or have held a position in an orchestra, the preparation must concentrate on the same six disciplines:

1. Careful choice and execution of the solo piece (a pianist is nearly always provided, and you will have to discuss tempi, etc)
2. The learning of as many excerpts as possible from the repertoire, preferably from memory, as the panel may suddenly wish to hear a well known passage that they have not provided the music for.
3. Sight reading practice.
4. Transposition (in all keys)
5. The steady build-up of stamina
6. Mental preparation and self-confidence.

If you are at college you will need the help of your teacher, who from his own experience, will advise you on the music that you might be asked to sight read. There are always excerpts that the panel can give you which you will definitely not know, but a careful study of all the excerpt books that you can find in the library, or may already own, and an equally careful study of the repertoire currently employed by the orchestra in question, whether it be opera or ballet music, will pay dividends. For the panel, it is often convenient to put up music that is readily to hand, as they can compare the candidates interpretation with those that they have recently heard in the orchestra. The excerpts that will comprise the sight reading may well be sent to you before the audition. This new and welcome development allows the panel to get a fair and balanced assessment of your general ability, without being prejudiced by any initial poor showing in this area.

PERFORMING EXCERPTS

Let us assume that you do not have the excerpts beforehand. You will be confronted at the audition by contrasting music, starting perhaps with Handel and Mozart where the demands are for a clean sound and neat classical phrasing, to Bellini, Rossini, Verdi, Puccini etc., where the accent is on lyricism and individual interpretation and from there on to Richard Strauss, and of course Wagner, where there will be a real chance to show off your technique over the whole range of the instrument, as well as a full sound and the ability to do some complicated transposition. The opening page of the third act of 'Arabella', is, for the first horn, difficult enough to sight read in F, – unfortunately it happens to be written in A! There are also some awkward transpositions in Verdi, particularly in the third and fourth parts. Some examples of the works that you may be asked to play in the audition, (I will give a slightly longer list at the end of the chapter), are: Sampson, Julius Caesar and Semele of Handel, Cosi fan Tutti and the Marriage of Figaro of Mozart, the Capulets and the Montagues of Bellini, Otello and Aida of Verdi, Rossini overtures and arias, any of the Operas of Richard Strauss and of course much from the Ring cycle, Lohengrin, Parsifal, Die Meistersinger and Tristan and Isolde of Wagner.

There are many famous passages which test the range of both the high and low players, as well as a number that make both play in unfamiliar areas. The high player must play low B flats and C's as convincingly as a low player in Rheingold and Gotterdammerung, also the second horn can be required to play well above the stave in Handel and other baroque works. If the orchestra is interested in you, they will want to see if your flexibility stretches this far. There are also several notorious hand stopped/transposed passages in Wagner that must be learnt; for example the fourth horn part in Gotterdammerung contains rapid transposition changes plus handstopping. One is often faced by a dilemma – namely whether to use a mute, the hand, or a sizzle mute. In view of this, advance work on these parts is essential, as the solos are often very exposed.

Basically get as much music 'under your belt' as possible. Buy or borrow as many excerpt books as you can. In order to practise honest sight reading, play your chosen passage through <u>only once</u> before proceeding to the next. Only when you have completed a series of excerpts, will you realise how proficient you are. At some auditions, you may only get one chance to demonstrate your sight reading potential. After you have read through the studies in this fashion, you can then go back and learn them properly. Try to discover the correct tempo and dynamics for the passage, listen to recordings and ask for advice. Having learnt the excerpts in this way, you may well be asked by the panel to play them in a completely different style. This is in order to demonstrate to them that you have the necessary flexibility and imagination for the job. Of course many of the points that have been raised apply equally well to orchestral auditions, the main difference being the repertoire involved.

With any luck, even if you are not successful in being offered the job, you may find yourself on the 'extras list'. This will quite possibly mean that you will have to come in and sight read a work under unfamiliar conditions. Never turn these chances down. If you arrive early and look at the part, asking your colleagues where the exposed passages are, it can be a very stimulating, (if on occasion hair raising), experience. Much stage band music is easy to play at sight, but still requires concentration. If you try to do your best, the rest of the section will appreciate your efforts and make you feel at home; moreover it will be another orchestra to add to your CV when applying for other positions.

SOUND

I must mention the need for clarity of sound. This is due to the acoustical restrictions of the pit itself, and the distance that the sound has to travel. An unclear sound will be lost before it reaches the audience. The sound of an Opera or Ballet orchestra tends to get better the higher and further that it reaches (just as the audience's view of the stage gets worse). Any distortion or lack of centre to the note will become exaggerated and have a detrimental effect at all dynamics. The panel will be looking out carefully for this at the audition, as a clear focused sound is a quality always associated by right-minded critics with the best players.

So many auditions are spoilt, not just by making mistakes, but by insufficient attention to general details of performance. Do not hesitate to ask intelligently at what tempo, dynamic etc. a passage should be played. Of course, if it is a passage that you really should know anyway, it will rather give the game away, but at least it will show that you are not overawed by the occasion, and are capable of showing a bit of initiative.

In a solo (say the one from Sonnambula), which demands a feeling for rubato and a Bel Canto style which matches that of the singer, you must be prepared to let yourself go a bit and show a theatricality and flair to match that of the stage. Remember though, it isn't just Opera which has a monopoly of rubato. Some dancers prefer tunes at different tempi, and one must always carefully watch the conductor for the last bar or two of every number, as there can sometimes be a long wait for the last note of a particular variation.

In a small audition room, it is very important not to compromise by keeping the dynamics down in relationship to the size of the room. You want to show the panel the complete range of your technique, in the time available. Don't play so quietly that it becomes a 'non dynamic', or so loudly that the sound begins to break up – clarity is all. Play your solo piece confidently and with sufficient character, (though no idiosyncrasies), as to distinguish your performance from the others. The general standard will be high, so that it will be not only technique but individuality, without eccentricity, that will mark you out as a possible candidate for the position.

A BRIEF SELECTION OF THE MUSIC THAT WOULD NEED TO BE PREPARED FOR AN AUDITION INVOLVING OPERA AND BALLET

AUDITION MUSIC FOR BALLET

1. All the Tchaikovsky ballets (useful practice for stamina) Viz. the last page of Swan Lake.
2. Romeo and Juliet (Prokovieff)
3. All the Stravinsky Ballet music:
    - The Rite of Spring
    - The Firebird
    - Petrushka
    - The Fairy's Kiss
    - Scenes de Ballet
    - Agon
    - Jeu de Cartes (card game)
4. Daphnis and Chloe (Ravel)
5. Nocturne from Midsummer night's dream (Mendelssohn)
6. L'après midi d'un faune (Debussy)
7. La Source (Delibes)
8. The Prince of the Pagodas (Britten)

Much of the modern ballet repertoire is choreographed to orchestral scores. It would be a good idea to check and see what the company has in its current repertoire. This can be done by telephoning the press and publicity office of the company concerned. The range of these works covers almost every era, from 'Pulcinella' and the Four last Songs of Richard Strauss to Mozart piano concertos. Unfortunately, excerpt books do not always include the most awkward or exposed passages. The complete versions of, for example 'The Firebird' and 'Romeo and Juliet' contain much, often difficult music that is not included in the orchestral suites. The only solution to this is to buy or borrow the full scores.

AUDITION MUSIC FOR OPERA

HANDEL — Julius Caesar
Sampson
Semele

MOZART — Idomineo
Marriage of Figaro
Magic Flute
Cosi fan Tutti
Don Giovanni

BEETHOVEN — Fidelio

WEBER — Der Freischutz
Oberon

BELLINI — La Sonnambula
I Puritani
I Capuletti e i Montecchi

WAGNER — Lohengrin
Meistersinger
Tannhauser
Tristan und Isolde
Parsifal
The Ring Cycle
Flying Dutchman (low horns)

BRITTEN — Peter Grimes
Turn of the Screw
Albert Herring

DELIUS — A Village Romeo and Juliet

TIPPETT — Midsummer Marriage (handstopping in 'Ritual dances')
The Knot Garden

JANACEK — Cunning Little Vixen
Katya Kabanova

STRAUSS — Der Rosenkavelier
Arabella
Cappricio
Die Schweigsame Frau
Salome
Elektra
Die Frau Ohne Schatten

		Intermezzo
		Daphne
BIZET	–	Carmen
VERDI	–	Aida
		Don Carlos
		Falstaff
		Otello
ROSSINI	–	Barber of Seville (overture)
		Thieving Magpie (overture)
		William Tell
		The Italian Girl in Algiers
		Semiramide (overture)
PUCCINI	–	Tosca
DONIZETTI	–	Lucia di Lammermoor
		Daughter of the regiment
LEONCAVALLO	–	Pagliacci

These are inevitably incomplete lists but will give you a base upon which to start your preparation.

THE HORN IN THE STUDIO

JOHN PIGNEGUY

JOHN PIGNEGUY

John Pigneguy was taught the horn by Neill Sanders, before continuing his studies at the Royal Academy of Music, with James Brown O.B.E.. During his time at the Academy, he won several prizes as a performer. Since then, he has enjoyed a varied and interesting career. This has included : 1st horn with the London Mozart Players, co-principal horn at

the Royal Opera House Covent Garden, a member of the Nash Ensemble, the Phillip Jones Brass Ensemble, and in addition has a wide experience of general freelance playing. John now specialises in studio recording for films, television, and all other aspects of session work.

He has been Professor of Horn at the Trinity College of Music, and in 1990 was elected an Associate of the Royal Academy of Music.

INTRODUCTION

The horn is probably one of the most versatile instruments, in that it fits into almost any musical combination. Ample testimony to this fact is the diverse kinds of music that the horn player can encounter in studio playing nowadays. The range of compositional styles include: symphonic playing, chamber music, contemporary-style music, solo playing, big band, dance band, jazz, rock, pop and easy listening. From this list you can see that studio work requires adaptability and flexibility.

PRACTICE AND PREPARATION

One of the first things studio work quickly teaches you, is that you usually have no idea what kind of music you will be playing on any given session until you actually turn up. Only then will you know if you are with a large orchestra, a small group, or on your own. The main prerequisite therefore, is that you are in practice and possess a reasonable set of 'chops'. There is nothing more embarrassing than turning up to a studio and having your lip 'go' before you have finished your warm-up, with a thick pad of music staring at you from the music stand. Some players may find it a nuisance to practice if they have two or three free days with a session at the end of them, but I decided long ago that I would prefer to do some regular practice and then discover that I needn't have done it, than not bother and get badly caught out.

My practice tends to consist of playing through pieces, or parts of pieces, aimed at improving stamina, flexibility, smoothness, technique, dynamics and sound. These pieces for example:

Franz Strauss Concerto
Cherubini 2nd sonata
Schumann Adagio and allegro
Strauss second concerto (1st and 3rd mvmts)
Horn trio from Brandenburg concerto No.1
(play it through with repeats, then once through without repeats and without stopping.)
Strauss 1 with almost no rest
Mozart Horn Quintet complete
Mozart 4 2nd mvmt. with no stops.

plus a modest amount of long notes, both loud and soft.

I usually practise for 30-40 minutes, rest for 20 minutes, then practise for a further 30 minutes. On a free day, I may repeat this sequence two or three times throughout the day. Remember, whatever and however you practice, always be constructively self-critical. I am also a great believer in taking a holiday now and then – it is vital physically and mentally to have a break, and I NEVER take my instrument or a mouth piece with me. Invariably I return refreshed, renewed and ready for the fray once more! However long or short the break, I always try to give myself sufficient time to get back into good playing shape.

ARRIVING AT THE SESSION

One of the advantages of a regular job, in a symphony orchestra for example, is that you are given an up-to-date schedule, you know from day to day exactly what music you will be playing and where, and (very important) <u>which</u> part. In the session world however, working (hopefully) for many different contractors or 'fixers' as they are known, there are no specifically set positions. Individual fixers, and possibly composers, may well have personal preferences as to who plays 1st horn, for example. Therefore, where you sit in the section may vary from session to session, and this uncertainty means that you should literally be prepared to play anything. Because of this, it is important to be well warmed-up and ready to play at the required time.

I like to arrive about 30 minutes before the start, and have a 10-15 minute warm-up, then go and get a cup of tea. Then I am ready to play.

My warm up starts with gentle middle-range slurring exercises, then I slur over the various harmonic series for two octaves and a third, starting on 'E' below middle 'C' (concert pitch) and go up in semitones to 'Bb' below middle 'C', plus some tongued scales and arpeggios. I try to finish with a few segments of tunes, just to get the sustained breathing going. If you are pushed for time, you will have to work out which parts of the warm-up are essential for you personally.

Always allow enough time, plus a little extra in case of delays on the way to work. If you look like being late, <u>NEVER</u> rush. You might arrive at the studio only seconds late if you do, but be so out of breath that you will not be able to play properly for a while; so just walk in normally even if the session has already started. If you are ever <u>really</u> late, you will discover the truth in the saying "Five minutes late they're cross, half an hour late and they're pleased to see you!" One important point about being properly warmed-up and ready, is that on some sessions, recording may start immediately with little or no rehearsal, so brain and lip need to be in gear from the start. This particularly applies to Jingles which usually only last an hour. On these sorts of sessions especially, good sight-reading is essential. Glance through the part and work out any patterns that may be in the music, possible scale or arpeggio-type passages, and make a mental notes of dynamics and phrasing.

CONCENTRATION

It is vital to keep your concentration going through recording sessions, particularly if there is a lot to play. Unless a 'hole-in-one' is achieved, it is quite likely that a piece will be recorded several times until it is right musically and technically, (fitting with a film, for example.) Concentration is required to make sure that you play your part right <u>every</u> time, as any one of the 'takes' might be the one that is going to be used. Time is money on sessions, and you do not want to be the one who "goofs" at a crucial moment, thereby taking the session into overtime. Of course, everybody makes mistakes from time to time and we all have off-days, but the more that you try and get things right, the more likely they are to be right. From a psychological angle I find that it helps me, especially if I have got something difficult to play, to assume that we will be recording the piece several times, even if I personally have not made a mistake. This means that instead of relaxing after a take, I keep my concentration going by preparing immediately for another, and not allowing myself to be distracted. Having a newspaper on the music stand alongside the music for example, or even on the floor where I can see it, tends to put me off. To avoid these visual distractions, I put any newspapers, books etc. under the chair and out of my sight-line.

STYLE

As I mentioned in the introduction, it is important to adapt your playing style to suit the music. You will not be much use if you play everything as if it were a Mahler symphony. The variety of playing that I have encountered in my career so far (including two years as 1st horn at Covent Garden, 20+ years with the Nash Ensemble, 4 years with the Phillip Jones Brass in addition to the usual freelance symphonic and chamber work), has made me acutely aware of the need to be flexible and, above all, to LISTEN to what is going on around me, to watch, and to anticipate.

In Opera, you have to listen to what the singers are doing as well as watching the conductor, and then play accordingly. In chamber music, trying to match the finesse and phrasing of the string and woodwind writing is vital for a performance to have any meaning. Brass ensemble playing requires that same approach, although due to the nature of the instruments, it is generally a more robust style of playing that is needed. The ten-piece brass group can be particularly taxing, as the lone horn has to compete with a full symphonic brass section of four trumpets, four trombones and Tuba. Under these circumstances, you have to learn how to pace yourself carefully. Playing in a symphony orchestra is a mixture of all the above, while the vast Symphonic repertoire calls for the greatest degrees of musical awareness and flexibility that you can produce. The much-loved and sadly- missed Tuba player John Fletcher, summed up all this awareness under the general title of 'Radar!'

Horn playing in a big-band or dance-band requires its own special 'Radar', because here, the playing style may make what is actually notated on the part sound completely different. The note lengths, phrases etc. will be totally dependent on the musical context; in many cases the notes on the page are just an indication of style and rhythm. Obviously here, aural awareness is vital. It is interesting to notice how much more meticulous the 'jazzers' usually are about note lengths, phrasing, ends of phrases etc., than we 'straight' players – we can often seem quite sloppy in comparison. Listen to good singers for breath control and phrasing, and listen to Heinz Holliger play Handel, (or anything else), on the Oboe to hear how it is done instrumentally.

SECTION PLAYING

Listening plays an important part in maintaining the balance of sound in section playing. The first horn is the leader, whatever you may think of his or her ability, and the dynamics of the section will be governed by how the first horn plays them. The same applies to both phrasing and note lengths. I have heard horn sections, where it was quite obvious that one player was taking no notice of what was going on in the rest of the section, with the result that the balance of chords and harmony parts was complete nonsense. Even though each player normally has an individual microphone, so that adjustments can be made afterwards during the mixing process, it is obviously much more satisfactory to get the internal balance right at the time of recording. Due to the acoustics of some studios – particularly the small ones – it is not always easy to hear the other players clearly, especially when wearing headphones. Listening to the playback of the first 'takes' will help you to correct any imbalance. One advantage of having individual microphones is that if there is a problem within the horn section, with a bit of knob-twiddling in the 'box', the culprit can be identified. This, as much as anything else, is an incentive to give of your best at all times.

Here are two useful tips on section playing, courtesy of my old professor, James Brown. When playing a unison passage that then splits up into, say, four-part harmony, all four players should play out a little more strongly in the divisi passage, so as to prevent the bottom dropping out of the sound following on from the strong unison. Tip number two concerns intonation, and Jim's idea, which I have found works very well, is that you can use a very slight, almost imperceptible vibrato where chords have not quite settled down pitch-wise. This trick helps to blur the edges of slight intonation problems, both within the section, and with other instruments. Used selectively this can be extremely effective.

PLAYING TO A CLICK TRACK

A lot of music for films, television and jingles is recorded using a click track, which is an electronic metronome fed to the player through headphones. This process guarantees almost total accuracy of timing, although there are some composers and conductors who prefer to work without a click. In addition to the click coming through the headphones, you can also have a variable mix of any pre-recorded track and/or the other players in the studio by asking the studio engineer for what you require. The headphones, more commonly known as 'cans', are worn with the left side on the ear and the right side off the ear. They should always be put on with the cable coming to the left ear - worn the other way round the cable will rattle on the bell. Early experience with playing to a click track might lead you to suppose that the clicks are speeding up or slowing down while you, of course, are playing perfectly rhythmically - I'll leave you to draw your own conclusions from this! Having to listen to a click with one ear and everyone else with the other is a useful discipline.

MUTES V. HANDSTOPPING

Composers generally know exactly whether they want a muted or a handstopped sound, and these instructions should always be adhered to. It does happen sometimes that, where handstopping is indicated, some players will use a mute, presumably to save having to transpose. This means that the sound of the section will be a mess and not the homogeneous sound that is required. To avoid this, practise handstopping in all registers – especially the lower one, as on your first sessions you will probably be covering a lower part and you do not want to get caught out. Some composers also ask for a metal or buzz mute. As this request can be unpredictable, it is worth carrying one as part of your everyday equipment.

ODDS AND ENDS

Synthesizers have been used for many years on sessions and they have an increasing variety of sounds and effects that players are required to play along with. Sometimes the actual pitch on a synthesizer track is hard to determine and therefore hard to tune to. The thing to do in this case is to go for an average pitch that is 'least bad'. The Jim Brown vibrato trick mentioned earlier can be particularly useful here.

Listening to the playback on sessions is very important in order not only to hear the accuracy of what you have just recorded, but to get the feel of the overall style of the music and also to decide whether or not anything needs to be played differently in order to fit in with that style. Record and film producers will have their own ideas about how the music should sound, and these in conjunction with the composer/arranger will give you all the information you will need to perform the piece, hopefully to their complete satisfaction. Remember though not to clutter up the recording booth unnecessarily during playbacks – you are there for a constructive purpose, not just to score points with the fixer.

Composers these days often start writing for films or records using a keyboard or synthesizer and a sequencer. Because of this, sometimes the horn parts are unplayable. Machines are capable of amazing things but they do not have to take a breath, and their lips don't get tired. The composer may also not fully understand the range of the instrument. Tact is sometimes needed to explain any problems that may arise as a result of this, and with care a compromise can usually be reached that not only keeps the original 'feel' of the music, but will allow the composer to agree that that was what he intended all along!

FILM SESSIONS

Film sessions work in three different ways; sometimes the composer will have timed the synchronisation of the music to film so perfectly, that he will not need to watch the film as the music is being recorded. In this case you will most likely just use the headphones with a pre-set click track. Some composers use a copy of the film on a video monitor beside their music stand, so that only they can see the film. Again you will have a click track in your headphones, although occasionally a confident conductor will work without it. The third option and from the players point of view the most interesting, is to project the film onto a large screen behind the orchestra, with the conductor following the action and trying to match the music to various markers, or 'streamers' as they are called, which are superimposed onto the rough copy of the film. Sometimes they will use a click track as well. As I mentioned before, time is money and the more aids that will speed up the recording process, the better.

When the music is recorded in this way, there can be a strong temptation to look over your shoulder at the action, and in the process perhaps mis-count the bars rest and lose your place. This is not advisable – there is plenty of time for 'player participation' at the end of the take, when the lights go down and the film and music are played back to check that they have the results that they want.

In the event of any tacet numbers, do not go out of the studio in case there is a sudden change to a different piece. Always check first with the principal horn to see what is happening. When you are sitting in the studio during a tacet number, keep still and quiet. Cover up your own headphones – put them over your leg, for example, if you are not wearing them, to prevent the click leaking into the studio and being picked up by the microphones. This can often be the cause of retakes and you do not want to be the culprit.

Some information about studios; the main ones that I seem to go to are (in no special order):

LANSDOWNE	–	Opposite Holland Park Tube
C.T.S.	–	Near Wembley Park Tube
HIT FACTORY	–	Behind Goodge Street Tube
SNAKE RANCH	–	Lots Road, near Chelsea Harbour
ANGEL	–	Gaskin Street, between Angel and Highbury and Islington Tubes
CARLTON TELEVISION	–	By Teddington Lock
BBC TELEVISION CENTRE MUSIC STUDIO	–	Opposite White City Tube
EMI ABBEY ROAD	–	Near St Johns Wood Tube

There are many other smaller studios dotted around London. The major studios either have their own restaurant/bar facilities, or else there are plenty of restaurants or sandwich bars nearby.

CHOICE OF INSTRUMENT

What sort of instrument is best suited to session playing? Players use a wide range of instruments and mouthpieces; Alexander singles, doubles, Bb/F altos – Conns – Yamahas – Paxmans. I use a Paxman model 40 Bb/F alto with an 'A' stopping valve (1974 vintage with the old large size bell) and a Halstead/Paxman Chidell 22A mouthpiece with a standard rim. I find this combination suits me best for session work.

PRACTISING BEING UNCOMFORTABLE

As playing conditions can sometimes be quite uncomfortable, and possibly unnerving, it is useful to have some idea of how to cope on such occasions.

Every player, even the most illustrious, gets nervous before a performance – a player with no nerves is not worth hearing. The control and channelling of this nervous energy is what should be aimed for, and slow, regular breathing exercises are a help in this respect. For example, breathe in slowly and deeply for a regular count of 10 seconds, really fill the diaphragm, (think of it like filling a balloon with air – a balloon fills up from the bottom) hold the breath for 3 seconds, exhale for 10 seconds, making sure all air is expelled, hold it for 3 seconds, then breathe in again slowly. Repeat this pattern as many times as required.

Jeff Bryant has a useful trick for practising being nervous. He suggests that you put your instrument down on a chair, go down one flight of stairs, run back up, pick up the horn, sit down and start playing (for instance, the Mendelssohn Nocturne, or the Tchaikovsky 5' slow movement solo, or the opening of "Oberon"). In this way you can fairly closely replicate not only the feeling of the heart pumping a little bit faster but also the slight breathlessness that a player may feel before playing such pieces.

On other occasions, you may be performing in a hot and sticky hall when, through general perspiration, the mouthpiece will not stay in one place. This situation can be practised by licking the mouthpiece rim, making it really slippery, then playing, for example, the Nocturne/Tchaikovsky 5'/Strauss 1, 1st movement with the mouthpiece feeling as if it wants to slide all over the place. It is quite possible to play normally at a concert under these conditions, but on the first occasion when this happens to you, you could easily feel completely "at sea", if caught unawares.

Michael Collins, currently (1992) the principal clarinetist with the Philharmonia Orchestra and a top soloist, told me that at his clarinet lessons when he was a student, his teacher would sometimes ask him to button-up his top shirt-button, pull his tie quite tight round his neck, switch on the electric fire in the room, get Michael to stand as close to it as possible, then play a concerto or two straight through. Michael said that he used to feel half-strangled, with the perspiration running everywhere as well, but his teacher was keen for him to experience the discomfort that can be felt when playing, before it actually happened to him.

Understanding a possible problem and knowing that you are aware of how to cope with it, is a great confidence booster.

GETTING INTO SESSION WORK

How do you get into session work? There is no set way but the grapevine of the freelance world seems to be quite effective, so getting yourself known is important. Read the 'get organised' section, and always remember that if you move or change your telephone number or answering service etc., you should circularise the details to all fixers (the Musicians' Union would supply details) regardless of whether they have heard of you or you have heard of them, or not. Don't forget – they need us as much as we need them!

ODDS AND ENDS

A few odds and ends; always use a pencil and rubber for marking parts – never a pen. The parts may be used again on another occasion, and different alterations might need to be made. Pick up and put down your mute quietly as the microphones pick up the slightest sounds – especially when you are close-miked. Likewise, when not playing, turn the pages of books, papers etc. quietly. Always keep a few seconds of silence at the end of a take; the reverberation of the last chord can take quite a while to die completely, and many otherwise excellent takes have been spoilt by a noise right at the end.

It is important to be of a personable nature and fit in with your colleagues generally. You may be the best player in the world, but if you are difficult to have around, you may find yourself with more spare time than you would like. Play well all the time, regardless of whether you like the music or not; your own contribution can make bad music sound good (and vice versa). In any case you have a moral obligation to always give of your best, as you are being paid for your services (you hope!)

GET ORGANISED

Use an efficient musicians' answering service to keep your diary. Always keep in regular touch with them. Use an answering machine on your home phone – preferably one that has a bleeper that will enable you to play back messages over the phone. I ring my machine a couple of times a day if I am out all day.

Once acquired, a bad reputation, either through personal unreliability or poor playing, is very hard to lose, so try to be as efficient and dependable as possible. This will help create a good impression, particularly important when starting out in the profession. This, together with a reliable approach to the job, will help to ensure a long and satisfying career.

GOOD LUCK!

SOLO PERFORMANCE & CHAMBER MUSIC

FRANK LLOYD

FRANK LLOYD

Frank Lloyd was born into a non-musical Cornish family in 1952. At the age of fifteen he joined the Royal Marines Band Service as a trombonist, but was subsequently changed to the French Horn. In 1975 he left the services to study at the Royal Academy of Music under Ifor James. After only three months, he was offered the

position of Principal Horn with what is now the Royal Scottish Orchestra. After four and a half years he joined the Royal Philharmonic Orchestra, remaining with them for three years.

During this period, his work as a soloist increased, and he left the R.P.O. to join the Phillip Jones Brass Ensemble, and subsequently the English Chamber Orchestra and the Nash Ensemble. Frank has been a professor at both the Guildhall, and Trinity schools of music.

This category of music making covers a large area, including Chamber orchestras, large chamber groups, wind groups, brass groups, orchestras playing for west end shows, horn ensembles, solo horn repertoire, and horn concerti. There must be more 'live' music performed under this category than any other. During your years at college, you will probably have been nurturing any connections that you may have established in the profession. These will most likely include some form of chamber music. This challenging field of music making can lead on to either a good source of regular work opportunities, or to a more permanent means of employment.

To start from the top, let us turn our attention to the largest groups of performers in this category, namely the chamber orchestras. Below is a list of those whose names come readily to mind:

> The Academy of St. Martin-in-the-Fields
> The English Chamber Orchestra
> The City of London Sinfonia
> The London Sinfonietta
> The London Festival Orchestra
> The Docklands Sinfonietta
> The Orchestra of St. Johns Smiths Square
> The London Chamber Orchestra
> The Sinfonia of London
> The London Sinfonia
> The Scottish Chamber Orchestra
> The Northern Sinfonia
> The Bournemouth Sinfonietta

Many of the names seem like variations on the same theme, but as far as I can tell, there don't seem to be any copyright infringement law-suits in progress at the present time! One step down the numerical ladder from the main chamber orchestras, we have the large, relatively full-time chamber ensembles, for example: The Nash Ensemble, the Manchester Camerata, London Brass and The Wallace Collection. This size category also includes the contracted orchestras/ ensembles for West End productions, with their truly diverse instrumentation.

When the numbers in a chamber ensemble get below about ten players, it naturally tends to become more specialised and the need for horn players diminishes accordingly! You may well have been a member of a brass or wind quintet during your years at college. These are good mediums in which to gain experience in small ensemble performance, but now you are hoping to <u>earn a living</u> playing the horn, so you will need to cast your net as wide as possible.

PLAYING STANDARDS

The standard of horn playing in this country is extremely high and, as seen in other sectors of the profession, this excellence is showing itself at a very early age. Having an abundance of natural ability may certainly help you in the technical aspects of playing, but still only puts you on the starting blocks of the race; a race that takes time and experience to learn how to run to the best effect. Yes, you might win a few times at the outset, but then things start to seem tougher, the pressure builds up, and your performance suffers as a result. It is said that there will always be work for good players. The most gifted of these may well get a head start over the majority of players leaving the colleges, as they will already have gained a reputation in the profession for themselves by the time that they leave.

It must be said at this point that many colleges do not look favourably on their students working 'outside', and can sometimes make it very awkward for them to take part in professional work. While I can understand the concern of the colleges that their students' academic work does not fall behind, I cannot condone any approach which would deny them valuable experience within the profession proper. There is also the argument sometimes voiced by players within the profession, that these students are taking away good work from players who might depend on that work for their living. This can be true to a certain extent, but it is doubtful that it could ever be on a scale that would undermine the chances of any good pro. getting work. I believe that you should get what contacts and playing experience you can while you are studying – it will help you in the transition between student and professional. Do not however, overstep the mark; there are many good players who have been drummed out of college prematurely on the grounds of disloyalty. You don't want to find yourself thrown in at the deep end before you really are ready to swim by yourself. A lot of valuable experience can be gained while you are completing your course.

So, the exceptional players may well have been working in the business regularly before they become full-time professionals, but what about all the other good players who have also reached the stage when they would like a slice of the cake?

'You don't have to be the best player to get the work' is a saying that is certainly true when it comes to working in London. An enormous amount of work of all kinds and for all levels of ability takes place there. There are plenty of opportunities for both freelance and permanent positions in other parts of the country too. It is up to you to decide first of all what course you would like your career to take: would you like to work in London or the provinces? 1st horn or 3rd? 2nd or 4th? Don't mind? Go for a job or freelance? want to teach as well? These are the kind of questions that you need to ask yourself.

HOW GOOD DO YOU HAVE TO BE?

Let us return to the question that was raised at the beginning of this section, 'How good do you have to be?' Being 'good' at playing the horn tends to be interpreted in many ways. The most significant one being how good you think you are, in relation to how good other people think you are. It goes without saying that an inflated opinion of one's own playing is a bad thing. It is after all other people who will hopefully be requesting your services, and it is their impression that counts. You must, of course, maintain a certain degree of self confidence and ambition, which are important factors in one's overall playing personality. Your playing standard is best judged by comparing it with those around you. In a college environment this might make you seem a star, but outside....? Suffice to say it is better to let your playing do the talking for you when it comes to impressing others.

Perhaps you now know how good you are in relation to your peers, but just how good do you have to be to make the grade? This is a question which cannot be answered easily, as you will have to cope with an enormous variety of situations in your career. We, as hornplayers, have individual preferences for certain things – high or low, fast or slow, slurred or tongued etc. etc. Your situation on leaving college will not be an easy one as you will have to be prepared to take on anything that might come your way. Aim to be as versatile a player as possible, the more versatile that your playing is, the more comfortable you are likely to feel in any situation, and that will allow you to play to your full potential (something that we all try to achieve), and this in turn will instil confidence into those who employ you, thereby increasing your potential for work.

ATTITUDE

Your general attitude and social bearing play an important part in enabling you to get on in the profession. Right from the earliest opportunity that you have to play in an orchestra, getting on with your colleagues will open doors for you that would otherwise remain closed. We all like to work with people who have a pleasant and amiable disposition – who wants to work with people that put over an air of unpleasantness, whether it be overbearing bullshit or just a pain in the neck! It all relates to being comfortable in one's environment. The job can be quite hard enough under the most favourable circumstances, and working regularly with someone who upsets the equilibrium is an added burden that can well be done without. There are many fine players in this profession, it is in your interest to keep on the right side of them.

FIRST INTRODUCTIONS

There are many ways that you might get your first introduction to the profession: through past colleagues, amateur/professional dates; your college professor; your own reputation, third party recommendation; doing auditions, (for extra work or permanent posts); being on a diary service; deputising, etc. Even asking to be put on someone's extra list will get them checking up on you. Getting maximum exposure will help your cause, and eventually, knowledge of your playing ability will seep through into the system.

With the help of their professors, outstanding students may get their first taste of real work as early as their first year at college, but generally speaking it will happen later in their studies. Understandably, you will have to win their complete confidence before you are given the opportunity to show what you are capable of. Amateur/professional dates are a good means of getting valuable exposure; the best players will stand out way above the others, getting people to notice and pass the news back. Being on a diary service will show that you mean business and are available and accessible at all times. Most of the other means of introduction will be based on the confidence in recommending you to others, that your playing inspires in your new colleagues. Believe in yourself, and gradually, if not speedily, your reputation will grow, and work will be forthcoming.

CHAMBER MUSIC

Now that we have established that you are an amiable and able player, how about getting some work in the chamber music scene? This is a quite legitimate target for your aspirations, but the challenges presented by living and working in a chamber group, are in some ways quite different from other music making activities.

Many of the demands are shared by the other disciplines: great powers of concentration, nerve, accuracy, and dynamic range. Particularly this last one, as blending in with the wind section might involve playing quieter than you ever thought possible. As second horn you will be required to perform the most frightening leaps from low to high, within a split second, (no pun intended), to emulate the first horn in as many ways as possible, (style, tuning, dynamics, etc) to play solo pedal notes longer than is actually possible, (work that one out), and often to play up to top 'B's and 'C's. Bear in mind that in a small ensemble everything that you do will be heard, there is nowhere to hide! Getting, (and staying), on top of these demanding technical challenges will give you a great deal of satisfaction. If this appeals to you, and the big orchestra scene is 'not up your street', then chamber music could well be the right outlet for your talents.

Although there are many chamber orchestras, it must be remembered that they only have two horns on strength at any given time, therefore they cannot match the volume of work being offered by the larger orchestras. This being said, they quite often increase their section to four horns, with the additional players being drawn from the extras pool. All principal horns receive requests for consideration regarding auditions and extra work. We consider all applications on their merit, and try to be as fair as possible. An introduction by recommendation helps, but even if your name is relatively new, a quick phone call to a colleague or two is enough to find out a little more about you. All it takes on your part, is to put a few details about yourself on a piece of paper, giving the name of your teacher etc., and send it either to the orchestral 'fixer', or the principal horn. The more good players we have on our books, the better. You will almost certainly be pursuing more than one avenue of work at this time, so try to stay in shape at all times – literally anything could arise at short notice, and you must be prepared to take any opportunity that comes along.

THE 'RIGHT' CHOICE OF INSTRUMENT

Rather than dictate what kind of instrument you should or should not play, I think that it is better to suggest an instrument that might be suitable for one's own style of playing. We each have our own ideas about what constitutes a 'good' sound and provided that the instrument plays well, with a variety of tone colour and dynamic control, the actual make is not particularly significant. Some principal players do insist, or certainly prefer their extras to play a certain type of instrument. If you wished to be considered for a permanent post in their sections, you might be advised to fall into line with the rest of the players; in fact you would probably want to anyway.

The 'right' instrument can depend on the repertoire that one is going to be playing. In a chamber orchestra with its lighter scoring, players will often opt for a B flat – F alto horn to assist them with the sometimes hair-raising horn parts. Even if they do not play them on a regular basis, you can be sure that they will have one tucked away somewhere. It is also a boon for the second horn, in view of all the 'leaping about', but I would not at this stage recommend the exclusive use of them in the initial stages of your career. Playing descant horns well takes a lot of experience, but in certain circumstances they are worth their weight in gold. When you have a better idea of the sort of job you would like to go for, you can start making hard and fast decisions about what instruments you want to stay with. Until then, bearing in mind the ease with which instruments can be traded in or sold, feel free to try any and every one of the arsenal of instruments that are available.

It takes a long time to work out what one's true likes and dislikes are; what seems like a golden opportunity now, might prove to be quite tedious in a few years' time. Falling into the rut of everyday drudgery encourages apathy, erodes ambition, and saps your ability to play to your full potential. These are the very reasons (coupled with an excessive workload), why the busier London orchestras can sound 'lifeless' and 'tired'. From that point of view, freelance work can offer you a variety of challenges that will keep you on your toes.

WHAT PLAYING CHAMBER MUSIC REALLY INVOLVES

I would like to concentrate on the finer points of chamber playing for instance: rehearsal technique, the role of the horn in various group formations, repertoire and the difficulties that arise therein. Chamber music is so named because it was designed to be performed in an intimate setting; it could thus be said that chamber music is "An intimate musical interaction between like-minded musicians". This intimacy is not something that can be achieved over a short space of time, it doesn't just happen if you throw a bunch of musicians together. In most cases it will take years to develop that true feeling of ensemble. It is the difference between playing the music as 'a group', and playing it with a unified musical understanding; with warmth, clarity and appreciation of the composer's wishes. You may spend a long time in a group sorting out the notes, but you will spend far longer perfecting these finer points of performance. Apart from obvious things like tuning, balance, dynamics and the straightforward technical demands of the music, there are considerations such as the uniformity of attack; how to match the attacks between the instruments? – who is going to lead that phrase to enable you all to play absolutely together? – how are you going to finish a phrase, breathe together, and accommodate each others' breathing requirements within the group? – articulate moving passages the same way? and having given consideration to all these factors, play MUSICALLY? These considerations I'm afraid, are all too often not awarded the importance due to them.

THAT EXTRA INGREDIENT

How many times have you been to a concert and come away at the end thinking "Yes, it was good, but it lacked something." It lacked the added ingredient that turns a good performance into a special one. Technical brilliance can be exciting and impressive, but unless musical aspect has been given consideration, it will end up sounding like an exercise and nothing more. Unfortunately this level of performance does not happen to any of us on a day to day basis, but the <u>striving</u> for it is what it's all about. You will probably remember performances that you have given, or concerts that you have experienced, that have hit that 'inner chord'. The sensation that gives you a thrill deep down inside, gets the hair standing up on the back of your neck, and sends shivers down your spine. When things are going well with your own performance and are giving you that sense of excitement, then you can be sure that it is having the same kind of effect on your audience too. You will not only hit the right chord in them, but will send them away duly impressed and satisfied. The time that a group spends in preparation and gaining a thorough knowledge of the repertoire, allied to the other points that are mentioned above, will eventually result in a musical style and character that is unique, and your reputation will be built upon this.

LEARNING THE DOTS

By learning the dots I really mean being aware not only of what you have to play, but also of what everyone else is doing in relation to your part. All the intimate shadings of nuance, tuning and balance, are only possible if everyone in the group has this complete understanding of the piece as a whole. This is especially important for the horn player in a wind ensemble, as it can be very easy to dominate in terms of the actual power of the instrument – you must know where and when to keep out of the way. Here the choice of instrument can help. If you insist on playing on an instrument that has a large unfocused sound, then you will find it difficult to play really quietly and the balance of the ensemble will suffer.

The brass ensemble has different problems, due to the forward facing trumpets and trombones having a natural advantage in terms of projection. A brass group will sound at its best playing within a wide variety of controlled dynamics, rather than a brash, constantly overblown one – that will lead to problems with tuning and stamina, as well as balance. A rich warm sound is the ideal to work towards, and is also much easier on the audience's ears over a whole concert's – worth of music. Even when you have to play flat out, you must not lose the overall quality of the timbre; 'blasting' will only distort and coarsen the sound. Conversely, if you can produce a _really_ quiet controlled pianissimo, as brass groups in general are not often heard to do, it will have a spectacular effect on your listeners. The beautiful hymn-like quality at these extremely quiet levels makes for a great showpiece; it is the contrast between this and the true, splendidly-controlled fortissimo, that will keep your audiences on the edges of their seats.

DYNAMICS

In a chamber orchestra playing mainly classical repertoire, horn dynamics need careful consideration. For instance, a _forte_ in a Mozart symphony will certainly not be the same _forte_ that you would play in a Mahler symphony! That might seem an obvious conclusion, but it is your responsibility as a member of the wind section, to exercise care regarding its overall dynamics. In most editions of the classical repertoire, scores are marked in a way that does not give any special regard to the horns. By this I mean that the same dynamic will be marked down the score for all the wind players. This can often cause balance problems if the horns do not modify their loud dynamics to match the rest of the wind section, or the orchestra as a whole. This considerate dynamic awareness sometimes results in chamber players being dubbed 'namby pamby' and being criticised for never 'giving it one!' I must say at this point, that it can sometimes be frustrating not being able to open up and do just that, but the ability to play quietly and with absolute control to match the rest of the wind, brings its own sense of satisfaction. There are in fact, many works that feature the horns and allow them to shine through, and you will get the chance to 'give it one' from time to time. Anyone can play loudly, but how many of us can play _really_ quietly?

The art is judging just the right dynamic for every situation; sustaining notes under the strings or wind so that you can be heard without intruding upon their lines, giving a little more to the lower note in an octave as it will not carry as far as the upper one, judging just how much to project a horn figure so that it stands out above the other winds, how to play a 'real' feature, etc., etc. All the time we should be coming out of the dynamic texture and blending back in again, timing our moments, and graduating the dynamics accordingly. One old 'pro.' once told me, "When horns are playing they should be heard". – Yes, but only in accordance with the requirements of the music.

TUNING

As you become accustomed to playing together as a chamber group, things will start to 'come together' more easily and more quickly. Tuning however, can still continue to be a problem, in fact it can be one of the most frustrating aspects of chamber music, and a constant cause for concern. In my opinion, it is the one factor that separates the really top class ensembles from the rest. Listen to the best groups, either instrumental or vocal, and you will immediately be aware of their impeccable tuning. No instrument is capable of being built completely in tune, and those fixed instruments such as the piano have to be tuned to a tempered scale, which is in fact a compromise, and the closest that can be achieved but which is far from perfect. Brass instruments are usually built very soundly, although many of the notes of the harmonic series are inherently out of tune. We, as horn players, are required to play higher in the harmonic series than any other wind instrument – for example most wind players rarely get off their 1st or 2nd harmonic, while we are required, even on modern instruments, to play up to the 16th! This, as we are all very well aware, presents us with problems due to the closeness of the higher harmonics, the natural acoustical gremlins (flat 5th, 10th harmonics) and the idiosyncrasies of each individual instrument, – flat notes, sharp notes, tight notes, uncentered notes, and just plain 'duff' ones.

It is a characteristic of all brass instruments that the more valves you put down, the sharper the resultant note is going to be. This is due to the fact that the valve combinations do not give exactly the correct length of tubing required to produce a harmonic series of the correct pitch. If it weren't for the fact that on a double horn at least, this problem can be partially eased by the use of alternately fingered harmonics and by using the 'F' horn, this would make life very difficult indeed for the poor hornist. Trumpets and tubas get around the problem by having a third slide trigger, (trumpet), and a fourth valve, (tuba).

Most of the tuning however is done with the lip, and to some extent with the hand in the bell. A good 'ear' is essential in this respect, as it is your inner sense of pitch that will determine what needs to be changed. For this to work effectively in a small group, all members have to be 'switched on' in the same way.

In many cases, it will not be sufficient just to play the notes where they normally are, – this might not work in respect of the overall tuning. At times you will have to bend notes a long way from where they normally sit, and often use alternative fingerings to achieve the desired pitch. Much depends upon the position of the note within the chord. Experience of the repertoire will enable you to play in tune within the harmony, and also when you have the lead line. Danger areas for the horn in the chamber repertoire lie in the thirds of keys such as: D major – (the C#), E flat major, (the D), concert D flat major, (the C) and B flat basso, (the A). These will all tend to sound sharp, especially as these notes can be a little on the 'bright' side anyway. To sound in tune, major thirds generally have to be played slightly flatter, as do minor sevenths. For chords with 'added' note harmonies, get the consonant chord in tune first; tune chords from the bass note, followed by an octave, then all fifths, then thirds, and then sevenths.

Atonal music will only sound at its best when all the dissonances are perfectly in tune. With discords, problems arise within the relationships of certain notes to others, and this can absorb a great deal of time in trying to perfect these finer points of tuning. A consonance played slightly out of tune might still sound acceptable, but a dissonance will be far worse. Experience will help you to 'play with your ears'. It will help in your practice sessions to play long, slow music. This will be hard work but it will assist you in the development of tuning awareness and also improve your stamina. Playing in tune when your lips are tired is even harder than normal.

TEMPERATURE

Temperature is an important factor, particularly relating to tuning with stringed instruments. Heat and cold affect these instruments in completely the opposite way to brass. In a very hot environment (TV studio for example), the strings of the instruments actually lengthen slightly, producing the obvious result of flattening their pitch, whereas when the air column of a brass instrument heats up, the air waves speed up making the instrument sound sharper, and so the gap widens.

You might think that the answer to this is simply to pull out your main tuning slide, but unfortunately it doesn't work quite as easily as that. Pulling out your main slide might get the open notes in tune but if the alteration is a large one, the fingered notes will not be in the correct relationship to the 'new' length of the main instrument (still with me?) consequently they will still tend to be sharp.

Now to the cold church!

After a few hundred bars rest in a choral work, picking up a cold instrument is akin to playing the first note of the day every time you do it. In addition to this we have the opposite problem to our hot environment, with the strings sounding sharper and the brass flatter. Pushing in all the main tuning slides might help slightly, but sometimes it is just not possible to push them in far enough. As if this wasn't enough, when you have been playing for a few minutes the instrument will start to warm up and sound sharper – flat one minute, sharp the next, who would want to play a brass instrument you might ask?

This dilemma is more acute for horn players, as the nature of the instrument requires us to have a very 'good ear' to be accurate when playing the upper harmonics – say third space 'C' upwards. Under these adverse conditions this 'good ear', which has taken years to develop can, in fact, let you down at the last minute. The reason is, that as the instrument cools and becomes potentially flatter, you are still hearing the general pitch of the musicians around you. Consequently, when you come to play your next entry, your internal pitch can be far removed from the pitch that your instrument is able to offer you, and a 'split' note will be the result through no fault of your own. Breathing hot breath down the instrument for a minute or two can help (I recommend a vindaloo!), but the whole affair can be very unnerving if you are not aware of these physical factors which are beyond your control. One answer is to play with like instruments, so you can all go down (or up) together! I remember once leaving my horn on a radiator to save having to do a warm-up, but when I returned, the instrument was so hot that I couldn't put the mouthpiece to my lips for five minutes and when I did, I discovered that I was at least a quarter-tone sharper than anyone else! Nevertheless, there _is_ something easier about playing a warm, sharp instrument than a cold, flat one.

THE PIANO AND THE OPEN STRING

One final word about tuning concerns playing with keyboard instruments. I am referring primarily to the piano, as that is the one with which most of us will have had some experience. In my experience you can either love it, or hate it. For example, your ensemble can spend ages getting the tuning just right, only for it to become relatively meaningless as soon as the piano joins in. The trouble is that the piano can't understand about flat thirds etc. and it cannot adjust itself to the finer points of tuning. You can't blame the player of course, (well you could try — let me know how you get on!), but even though it can upset relative tuning within an ensemble, the fact is that it usually plays a great deal better in tune than most groups. However much we might feel that our own tuning is the correct one, <u>we</u> can use our ability to compensate and adjust the tuning; it cannot. A similar problem can arise with the use of <u>open strings</u> on the violin family. They can occasionally sound very out of tune in some keys. I say <u>can</u> because it does depend which part of the chord the offending note is positioned. One good example of this is the last chord of the first movement of Mozart's horn quintet. The second viola has a double stop with a low 'G' having to be played on an open string. It is consequently never quite flat enough to sound in tune, (it is the third in the key of E flat major); – you will undoubtably be able to cite many others.

RUNNING YOUR OWN GROUP

In your efforts to perfect your ensemble, one thing is worth bearing in mind; not all players are of the same standard and have the ability to bend notes to fit them into the chord. You have to accept that your own notes will not always be where you want them to be either. If you have a member of a group who is having so much trouble holding his/her own, that the group is prevented from sounding its best – and it only takes one player – then you may have to consider a change of personnel. A very diplomatic approach is required here for obvious reasons, but it is infuriating for the rest of the group if someone is 'rocking the boat'. Even if it means undoing untold hours of work to have to start afresh with a new player, in the long run it will be beneficial to all concerned.

Groups formed within the confines of the colleges face their toughest challenge when the time comes to leave and make a living within the profession. Being able to keep the same personnel can be a major factor in success or failure. Most ensembles formed at college disband during or soon after finishing their final term. This is not surprising, as there are bound to be conflicting interests as you all strive for work in your own areas. Difficulties will arise in the allocation of rehearsal time, maintaining commitment, fulfilling engagements, and even just staying in the same city. The most important aspect is how much time and effort you, as individuals, are prepared to put into the group.

Attracting work which pays well is, after all, what we are all trying for! Contacts can be made through getting yourself some exposure: concerts at college, competitions, private sponsorship, (for a Wigmore Hall concert?), Barbican foyer? If you want to succeed, in fact, if you are <u>determined</u> to succeed, then you will have to put in a lot of 'spade work' to make it happen. It is a very competitive business and there are many others out there trying to do the same thing, get the same work and the same sponsorship. What you have to do is offer a product of distinction (maybe packaged slightly differently?), which you can deliver consistently, in an exciting way, and which will encourage influential people to put their, (or other peoples), money behind you. There is no easy way of going about this, but if you have a competitive spirit, the challenge will be worth it. Don't give up easily, stick it out through the hard times, and the best of luck to you!

THE BRASS QUINTET

These days, many groups, (primarily brass), have taken to performing on stage over and above the demands of the music. This can be a very successful means of appealing to a wider audience. The most prominent groups in this field are: Canadian brass, The Brass Band and Empire Brass. As their choreographed antics have proved to be so popular, they in turn have spawned many look-a-like groups in their wake. A word of warning about emulating this kind of performance – these are FULL TIME groups in that kind of work, and they spend many, many hours with a choreographer on some of the routines which they perform. This sort of approach is unfeasible for the majority of us, but a small amount of stage antics can have a good effect, provided that they are tasteful, well done and subtle. Presentation is very important, as anything that looks ad-hoc or shabby will cheapen your whole performance. One problem is the effect that any 'theatricals' will have on the musical side of the performance. Leaping around on the stage is inevitably going to detract from the music, so good programme planning is essential. Even Canadian Brass occasionally sit down to perform a difficult piece and apart from making it easier for themselves, it allows the music to have the full attention of the audience. Playing standards can suffer dramatically within a choreographed routine, but if the act is good, then that should make up for it. Basically, if you can't do it well, leave it out. There are other ways to get an audience on your side.

Starting with a good strong opening, which you could do from memory and/or standing up, is a good opening gambit. Break down the 'us and them' barrier by introducing pieces even if there are programme notes. A small amount of 'off pat' humour is good, if you feel that the audience will appreciate it. This includes humour within the music – i.e. Joseph Horowitz' Music Hall Suite. It is generally better, however, to leave the jollies until the second half of the concert, as they will have a better effect then. Playing from memory takes an enormous amount of time to prepare, but if you know the music inside out, then the performance can take on a new and exciting dimension. There will, however, be venues which will prefer a straight and formal concert, and will turn up their noses at any 'fooling about'. Try and find out as much as possible about the wishes of the organisation beforehand: formal/informal, middle of the road music club, strong youth element, over 60's club etc.. Tailor your programme to suit any occasion; your ability to please will assist you in getting a return date.

ABOUT PRACTISING

Playing at the quietest of dynamics can (and does) frighten the best of players. It is not a comforting feeling, when settling down to rehearse a Haydn symphony after a very heavy or loud concert the night before, you find that the only dynamic at which notes will speak properly is mezzo forte! This is something that happens to all of us at one time or another; conversely after many hours of playing quiet dynamics, the loud playing suffers accordingly. The only way to prepare yourself for the coming day is to PRACTISE. There can be many reasons for not practising: fatigue, lack of incentive or enthusiasm, lack of work – nothing to practise _for_ – too many other things to do, need a lie – in, do it later in the day etc. etc. etc. I have heard them all including "I couldn't face the noise", or just plain "I've got duff chops". I wonder if the reason for the duff chops ever occurred to the player? But to give these excuses some credit, there can be problems associated with finding a place where one can practise undisturbed. I am constantly enraged by the continued lack of practice facilities at most of the well known music colleges. For many students it is just not possible to practise at home because of consideration for the neighbours. This can mean waiting for hours to secure a room at college, or simply not bothering to do any out of sheer frustration. I sympathise with students over this, but I do stress that even the smallest amount of practice is important. Even ten minutes first thing in the morning will make things that much easier for you when you come to play later in the day.

THE OBJECTIVES OF PRACTICE

Practice is a very personal thing. Each of us has over the years, developed a particular type of warm up routine that sets us up for the rest of the day. It is not the warm up routine that concerns me, however, but the practice period immediately after the warm up, when the good work can be done. To play in control quietly, in the high register and to sustain this quieter level of dynamic required in a chamber orchestra you need good stamina. Not the same kind of stamina that enables you to blast through a Mahler symphony, it's a bit more subtle than that. There is no better way to practise than to run through the kind of playing that you will be experiencing, and in this instance, that means concentrating on long held notes – remembering the SUPPORT coming from the diaphragm, (all too easily forgotten). High, slow slurs, (pianissimo), between notes of varying intervals, moving both up and down, concentrating on keeping the gap between the notes clean and controlled. Also, experiment with different fingerings over different intervals, remembering, (apologies if this is too technical), that slurs will respond more favourably when moving from an even numbered harmonic, to another even numbered one – likewise from an odd to an odd – especially in the middle–low register (middle G to low G). Do not neglect the flexibility studies and lip trills, as they will help you build the very flexible embouchure that you need for this sort of work. Once again, unfortunately, there are not short cuts to achieving these ends, hard work will reap benefits – but that's the same story the world over! I mentioned earlier that the standard of horn playing today is exceptionally good, but with so many fine players around, what are the chances of making a solo career? Having had the opportunity to play a few concertos at college, does not unfortunately give you the necessary qualifications to launch yourself into a solo career. It <u>will</u> do your credibility a lot of good, and you will be recognised as a player with potential, but don't let those few moments of glory go to your head! The reality of the situation can dishearten even <u>the</u> most ambitious of players. The truth is that these days, being a full-time soloist on the horn, is not a viable proposition.

BEING A SOLOIST

When talking about horn soloists, the name Barry Tuckwell immediately springs to mind, as being a legend in the solo horn world. If you look back at the circumstances that brought him to fame and a solo career that has lasted in excess of forty years, you will see that things have changed a lot since he started out. Firstly, and most importantly, Barry has a prodigious talent for playing the horn and during his years in London as principal with the London Symphony Orchestra, he nurtured his solo career and capitalised on the fact that there were very few other people doing it in the world at that time. By getting his unique talents down on recordings he built an unassailable reputation for himself, a reputation that we all now admire and look up to. He is an inspiration to the exceptionally fine young players who are regularly appearing these days. This is great for the profession generally and maintains the tradition of fine horn-playing that we have in Britain. It also means that all the solo work on offer has to be shared out amongst the talent that is around. Other than Barry, there is not one other player in this country who earns a living solely from playing horn concertos and even he is diversifying more into conducting these days.

We are fortunate to have so many fine players and soloists in this country, as they offer a variety of styles and abilities to suit all tastes. For that reason I don't think that there will ever be any one person monopolising the soloist scene in the future. In countries where classical music is held in higher esteem than in Britain, there will be many more solo opportunities and for that reason, many very talented American and English players make a career for themselves abroad - I am thinking particularly of Germany. It is a fact that we are the poor relation of Europe in this respect. Our woefully inadequate government subsidies create less than ideal working conditions, with little or no security. The ridiculous work schedules and heavy touring commitments that many orchestras have to undertake, create stress at home and undermine one's confidence through sheer fatigue. Things are beginning to improve, but in London especially, we still have to work far harder than our European counterparts to make a decent living. To be able to break into the European market, you will need an exceptional 'track record' with preferably some recorded material in your CV. Best of all would be to live in the country concerned, or be a native of that country.

WHAT A SOLOIST NEEDS

All this aside, there are certain prerequisites before you even attempt to "have a go" at the solo scene. One of the major assets a solo player needs is to have a good command over the complete range of the instrument, with emphasis on the high register. Even an excess of technique is desirable — that extra virtuosic prowess can help you when playing under pressure, (in front of a few thousand people etc), so that, if/when nervousness sets in, you have a little bit extra up your sleeve. Also, having a technique that is rarely under strain will enable you to express more of your personality through the instrument, and get you away from the undesirable aspect of just note-getting. A good nerve is important, for as we all know, being nervous is one of the most common reasons for not playing at one's best. There are many tried and tested ways in which one can tackle the nerves problem: certain drugs for instance, (most commonly 'Beta-Blockers'), and/or alcohol. These have the inherent dangers of dependency and the false sense of security that they provide. We are not fully aware of the long term effects of drug taking, but the effects of alcohol abuse are all too plain; and in many cases being responsible for wasted talent; embarrassment, frustration for one's colleagues, losing friends and, in the end, premature retirement from the profession and long-term damage to one's health.

It is the false sense of security brought on by alcohol which gives one the belief that everything coming out of the bell of the horn is wonderful, (although some people believe this even when they are sober!) when, in fact, the truth is just the opposite. The impaired sense of awareness and sluggish reactions can result in fumbled technique, shortening of phrases, memory lapses and a host of other related effects. The greatest danger is the fact that, although alcohol may seem to have a calming effect on one's nerves, this is short lived, and the alcohol in turn creates more stress as the body works harder to rid itself of the toxins. What then happens as the body starts building a resistance to alcohol, and its tolerance of it increases? Yes, more drink is needed to get the same effect, and one is truly on that slippery slope.

Social pressures might mean that some drinking is a part of the job for a brass player, and many players do have a small drink to steady the nerves just before a concert. As long as you keep this under control, then no harm will be done. Neither drink, nor drugs, offer a long-term solution for nerves, and although a small amount of nervous apprehension can be good for you, most forms of it are detrimental to one's performance. Nervousness stems from a variety of sources: tension through stress caused by stage fright; lack of confidence caused by not being in full command of the technical requirements of the concerto undertaken; or lack of preparation either regarding the memory; or the stamina, (in other words practise) etc.. Other factors to consider are problems with pitch; an uncomfortable environment, (too hot or cold); duff accompanying orchestra; bad acoustic/stage etc.. Most of these can be overcome with experience, but they can all be responsible for unnerving you and undermining your confidence.

PREPARING FOR A SOLO PERFORMANCE

Lets face it, even with a great set of chops, loads of technique, great sound and stamina, it is never going to be easy playing concertos, and Barry Tuckwell would be the first to agree. It is the awareness that comes through preparation which is the key; keeping yourself on top of all the demands is essential. Learning concertos from memory is one such preparational task, and although it may seem daunting at the outset, you can achieve good results in a short space of time. With a bit of application, even the most difficult concertos can be learnt. Play along with a recording and get to know the orchestral cues etc., so you don't have to rely on counting blind bars rest. Physical fitness and mental awareness are inextricably linked, and it is the mental concentration that can override a lot of the problems – in everyday life as well as playing the horn! Relaxation to overcome the tension that causes the shakes, and deep breathing, (not too vigorous,) should help to steady those nerves.

To summarise: work yourself out a regime of practise and preparation, starting a week or so before the concert, (longer if it's a new concerto). It is a good idea to get it all going well, and then come back to it closer to the date, to work on the finer points of the performance. Include exercises for stamina building, memorising, (not absolutely essential but expected these days), and playing right through the concerto to get the true feel of pacing yourself. Good stamina builders to use on any occasion are: 1st and 2nd movements of Mozart 4; 1st page Strauss 2nd concerto, the Nocturne from Midsummer Nights Dream and any movement from Othmar Shoeks concerto. Don't overdo it by trying to play on caved in chops. Play until you feel the face tightening up, then play a little more in an easier register, and a few low notes to warm down, then leave it for a while and come back to it later in the day. This way you will build up the stamina in stages – continued playing on very tired chops can wreck them for days if you are not careful.

You will understandably want to play as well as you are able on the day, (and every day), so this preparation is essential. The confidence that it will give you will enable you to ride over the difficulties that are just waiting to drag you under! It is logical that the more you play a certain concerto, the more familiar you become with it, not just in terms of memory. Experience will show you where the problems lie; – pacing yourself to save something for the big moments or high passages, using the acoustic to your best advantage; 'riding' the orchestra; knowing when to be 'sotto voce' as well as coming to the fore, and most of all, <u>playing to your strengths</u>.

One last thing to bear in mind about solo playing; it will stand you in good stead to spend a few years in an orchestra before making such a move. There is more to be gained from that experience than any other. It gives you the discipline of section playing, as well as experience in control of dynamics, especially at high volume! You will hear other players play concertos; take in what you like about their performances, they may even inspire you! As principal of an orchestra, you will get opportunities to perform concertos with them and you will by virtue of being in the profession proper, get your name more widely known and increase your potential for all the other forms of work offered to a recognised player – you do not have to be a principal to get a good reputation for yourself.

GETTING AN AGENT

If you are keen to "have a go" at the solo scene, get an agent to work for you. Agents come in a mixed bag of good, bad and indifferent, and you would be well advised to get someone to work for you on a personal level in a small agency. One of the big problems stems from lack of work in this country, as the horn will never have the attraction of the violin or piano, nor can the concerto repertoire match the range and volume of the countless works for these popular instruments. We can at least be thankful to Mozart and Strauss for their contributions, as they will always be challenging, and no two performances will ever be quite the same. They are the 'staple diet' of our repertoire, and although there are many other solo horn works which offer challenges over and above the Strauss concertos; Britten Serenade, Haydn 1, Othmar Schoek etc., you can be sure that nine times out of ten, you will be asked for Mozart 4, or Strauss 1!

PLANNING A RECITAL

Most of the solo work that any of us get in the early years, is usually in the form of recitals (unless you are fortunate enough to have won "Young musician of the year"!) The preparation for a full length recital is in some ways harder than for a concerto. Other than memorising all the pieces – although you can if you like – you will have to develop a very strong pair of 'chops'. We have already talked about the way to do this. The very heavy workload that a recital presents, can be alleviated to a degree by good programme planning; interspersing the more difficult pieces e.g. Adagio and allegro with less tiring ones, such as Berceuse (Damase), or the Beethoven sonata. Introducing each work helps, as it breaks down the barriers between you and your audience, and gives your lip a chance to rest. Even printed programme notes, some other relevant information or anecdote about the composer, or the piece itself, will help to keep the audience interested.

Plan a good mixture of contrasting pieces, but remember that if you include short pieces which might be played in quick succession, then you will have to consider how drastic the key change will be between them. Related keys, or those that do not 'jar', are easier on the ear. One such pairing that I do, is the father and son duo of Franz and Richard Strauss. After playing Franz Strauss' nocturne, I go without much ado into the Andante of Richard. The subtle change from the rich key of D flat, to the bright 'open' key of 'C', has the effect of opening a door and letting in light, which is quite astonishing, and it works as a wonderful contrast. Plan your programme also, so that the weaker elements are not left on their own, for instance, at the beginning or end of a half.

A complete programme of horn music is a lot for anyone to listen to, so consider asking your accompanist to include a short piano solo in each half to relieve any potential boredom. Bearing the boredom factor in mind, it is wise not to make the programme too long. Keep the printed programme on the short side, save something in your chops for the end, and have a couple of razzle-dazzle encores up your sleeve to send them home glowing.

A lot of careful preparation goes into a recital, not the least of which is choosing a good accompanist! They are worth their weight in gold. It is true art to be able to accompany in a sympathetic way and to 'stick with you' under all circumstances. When you know that yours is capable of doing this, you will have one less thing to worry about.

THE PROVINCES

Although most work opportunities for the freelance and job seeking horn player are naturally centred around London, which has the highest concentration of work in the music field, there are a great many opportunities to be had in other cities around the country. People will tell you that the provincial orchestras are the training ground for many London musicians. You only need to look around at some of the London horn players to realise how many spent time in the provinces; Geoff Bryant, (Bournemouth Symphony); Hugh Seenan; (Scottish National –now called the Royal Scottish Orchestra, whose past principals include Barry Tuckwell.) Michael Thompson (BBC Scottish); Julian Baker, (Halle Orchestra), and many more, past and present, who have passed through these orchestras and others on their way to London.

These days provincial orchestras can offer an attractive alternative to the 'rat race' of London and in many ways are a better proposition altogether. For a start they offer the security of a salaried post, (hard to come by in London); they will cover all the repertoire that you will find anywhere; and give you concerto opportunities on which to build your reputation, and finally offer you, in most cases, a living and working environment that most 'town bound' musicians would envy. The salaries in these orchestras are excellent by any standards, and offer more in real terms by virtue of the fact that the cost of living is generally lower when taken overall. You must also take into consideration the fact that free time, (governed by on-call hours per week, and a standard part of any players contract outside the London self-governing orchestras), usually amounts to two full days per week with more time off in lieu of extra hours worked. These factors combine to form such an acceptable lifestyle, that some players choose to settle down and make their careers in the provinces. The only thing that could be construed as being a disadvantage in not being in London, is that one can get out of touch by not being 'close to the action' and possibly lose out on work which might further one's reputation in London itself. On the whole though, the experience and experiences that you will gain from a provincial post, will far outweigh the disadvantages. You will get opportunities to do things that would rarely be offered to you so early in your career if you were in London.

There is usually a regular turnover of young players, and one important factor is that compared with their London counterparts, provincial orchestras make a point of advertising their vacant positions in the national press, and although the applications are vetted, (by the principal horn usually), the BBC orchestras at least have a policy of hearing all the applicants.

THE ADVANTAGES OF A PROVINCIAL JOB

It is sometimes thought that leaving London means saying goodbye to first-class music making, but this is complete nonsense. The orchestras outside London can be as good as the best on offer anywhere else. It is often complacent London based musicians who get a shock when they hear a provincial orchestra 'on song'. However, one thing about London musicians is their ability to sight-read very well, since rehearsal costs are very high, and there is a pressing need to keep these at a minimum. Some well known conductors have turned down opportunities to conduct in London when their demands for extra rehearsal time could not be met. In provincial orchestras the rehearsal time is most frequently at the beginning of the week in preparation for a series of performances over the latter half of the week and the weekend, but this will vary from orchestra to orchestra depending on recording commitments etc. BBC orchestras give greater emphasis to studio recording, and most of their public concerts are recorded for future transmission. Generally speaking, there will usually be two full days of rehearsals before a public concert depending on the repertoire. 'Repertoire' in this sense purely means <u>which</u> pieces are being played, rather than in its other context used throughout this book of 'pieces which are played more frequently than others'. This is an important difference, as one orchestra's 'repertoire' will never exactly correspond to another. Rest assured though that the 'standard' orchestral repertoire of the symphonies of Beethoven, Brahms, Tchaikovsky, Mahler etc., will present you with exhilarating challenges time after time. You certainly need to have a good knowledge of these composers when you audition.

After a few years in the provinces, you, as a young ambitious player, may start to cast your eyes towards London, but by this time you will be a much more prepared, experienced and able player, (experience makes a better player), than ever before. Speak to any of us who have lived and worked in the provinces, and I think you will find that all of us gained a great deal from the experience. You will have the opportunity to learn the job of playing the horn in a less pressurised and amiable environment than the intensive, stressful and impersonal atmosphere that is often associated with London.

For your information here is a list of all the orchestras outside London along with their principal players (as at the end of 1992).

SCOTTISH CHAMBER ORCHESTRA, Edinburgh
Robert Cooke

BBC SCOTTISH SYMPHONY, Glasgow
David Flack

ROYAL SCOTTISH ORCHESTRA, Glasgow
David McClenachan

ROYAL LIVERPOOL PHILHARMONIC, Liverpool
Johnathan Barratt

NORTHERN SINFONIA, Newcastle
Peter Francome

BBC PHILHARMONIC, Manchester
Jonathan Goodall

HALLE ORCHESTRA, Manchester
David Cripps

CITY OF BIRMINGHAM SYMPHONY ORCHESTRA
Claire Briggs

BBC WELSH SYMPHONY, Cardiff
David Lloyd

BOURNEMOUTH SYMPHONY
Richard Thomas

BOURNEMOUTH SINFONIETTA
(Post vacant at time of writing)

GENERAL FREELANCE WORK

PAUL PRITCHARD

PAUL PRITCHARD

After a brief period in the National Youth Orchestra of Great Britain, Paul Pritchard studied the Horn at the Royal College of Music with Douglas Moore. Shortly after the completion of his studies, he joined what is now the Birmingham Royal Ballet as principal horn. Two years later he joined the English National Ballet where he stayed for seven years.

It was during this period that he began to build up the network of freelance contacts which now employ him full-time. These include the main Symphony and Chamber orchestras, in particular the London Symphony Orchestra, with whom he has travelled extensively, Glyndebourne and English National Operas, recording for TV, film and advertising, as well as many London musicals. He is also a member of the Orchestra of St. John Smiths Square.

'Freelance' can be taken to mean several different things. Most players experience a kind of freelancing during and just after, their term at college or university. Few instrumentalists are lucky enough to move directly into a full-time job, which means that most of them have to take the first steps in a difficult career entirely on their own. Few if any players leave college with the sole intention of freelancing; however the actual number of full-time jobs within the profession has been steadily declining over the past few years. This means that, not only do people tend to stay longer in a particular job, but also, young players face the prospect of having to wait several years before being able to audition for the kind of job which they find attractive. It is quite possible that at some time during that period, they might find that they would prefer to freelance for the rest of their career.

There can be no doubt that the repertoire and relative security offered by a full-time job has many initial advantages over the uncertain world of the freelance player. Against these must be set such factors as the heavy and highly-pressured schedule that most orchestras have today. You would be working with the same people day in, day out and under these conditions your strengths and weaknesses would become quickly apparent to all. A great deal of internal politics, which can often be very unpleasant, are an almost inevitable part of the job. After weighing up all these factors, some players find that they would prefer to remain independent. Having decided to remain independent the following options present themselves:

1. To build a career as a freelance player – this might include a certain amount of teaching and other activities such as arranging/composing.
2. To concentrate on teaching.
3. To leave the profession altogether.

This chapter concerns the main kinds of work that you will encounter in the course of your first few years as a freelance player – except studio playing which has a chapter all of its own.

TOURING OPERA AND BALLET

Many musicians find that their first regular freelance employment comes from one of the touring Opera or Ballet companies. These cannot in general be regarded in the same category as full-time jobs, as they are seldom active for more than a part of the year and with the exception of the Birmingham Royal Ballet, do not guarantee any employment.
The main companies in this category are:

> The Birmingham Royal Ballet
> English National Ballet
> London City Ballet
> Northern Ballet
> Scottish Ballet
> Ballet Rambert
> London Contemporary Dance
> Glyndebourne Touring Opera
> Opera Factory

Not all of these use full-sized symphony orchestras. Some of them use scaled-down versions of the repertoire with specially commissioned contemporary chamber works, as well as taped music.

A position with most of the established companies will usually be awarded on the basis of an audition, followed by a trial for the successful applicants. If you are fortunate enough to be selected for the job, you will be offered the schedule whenever the company needs an orchestra. This will vary from only a couple of months for the smaller companies, to over three quarters of the year in the case of the Birmingham Royal Ballet.

As in any orchestra, the section principal will have the strongest influence over any new appointments or the choice of extra players. The orchestra may well also have its own committee. Many of the players in these orchestras will regularly work elsewhere and this creates a substantial amount of work on a daily or weekly basis. Although most sections have their regular deputies who are familiar with the repertoire, as they are often away from their home base, there is a constant need for new players.

As in any form of freelancing, the important thing is to get on to as many orchestral managers' lists as possible. One way is to write directly to them care of the company office, giving all the relevant details about yourself for them to file away. If a post were to become vacant, you might find that they would approach you even if you have not already written in. If you do not get the offer of a job, a good audition or even a fair one will almost always put you on the shortlist for extra work. Another way is to telephone or write to the section principal and tactfully introduce yourself. He/she probably won't be able to do any more than offer to put your name on the bottom of his or her list but it will make them aware that you are interested in working with them.

COPING WITH THE JOB

Excellent sight-reading is indispensable to a freelancer and you will find that it will be put to the test when you have to read a show in performance, that the rest of the orchestra know well. Most of the ballet repertoire is fairly straightforward for the horn, with the notable exception of some of the twentieth century works, which are listed in Julian Bakers chapter. The main area for drawing unwelcome attention to yourself though, is by failing to follow the many tempo changes, pauses and general pauses that are an integral part of the performance of Opera and Ballet. Very often these are not printed in the score but pencilled in the part to follow the choreography, or a particular singer's interpretation. BEWARE OF THESE! Sometimes they are not even marked in the part, as the regular players are so used to the piece, that they follow them automatically. After a while you will develop a 'sixth sense' about where these occur.

When you are going to sight read an Opera or Ballet, make sure that you arrive early enough to have a good look at the part, noting not only any solos or tricky-looking passages, but pauses and 'tramlines' and passages that appear to have significant or sudden tempo changes. However well that you play technically, if you perform a loud and unsolicited solo, you will leave wondering why you bothered to play the horn in the first place. Asking a member of the section to point out the pitfalls is a good idea, but remember that there may still be things in the score which they take for granted, that might prove awkward to sight read.

Many ballets, particularly the Tchaikovsky ones are very long and tiring. Regardless of the volume being generated by the rest of the section, if you are not used to long loud blowing, you would be well advised to pace yourself – especially if you are doing two shows in one day. After a few shows you may find that this kind of playing begins to affect your lip. You can offset the effects by a fairly long, gentle mid-register warm up and by a short and gentle 'warm down' after the show. In many ballet scores, the horn parts contain little except for harmonic padding but this can be more tiring than any of the big tunes in the orchestral repertoire. The danger is that you can become bored and forget such vital things as diaphragm support, deep breathing and just concentrating on your technique and blowing right through the instrument. Obviously if what you are playing contains little or no thematic content, it is hard to keep interested. Unfortunately the deterioration in your technique usually only reveals itself when you return to the more demanding world of orchestral performance. Once you have struggled with the realisation that you have acquired a set of lips that can only play loudly in the middle register and you are expected to turn in a delicate performance of 'Siegfried Idyll' that night, you begin to realise the importance of treating both ballet music and lips with the greatest respect!

With these companies, it is quite possible that your first date will be on tour. Unless there are any rehearsals or matinees, most of your day will be free. The increased time that you spend with your colleagues means that they will have the opportunity to assess you socially. Like it or not most brass players gravitate towards the pub – particularly on tour. If you do not wish to join them this can be a handicap. Obviously you do not have to drink alcohol but if you do, make sure that you do not get pressed into drinking more than you can handle. When you are in a relaxed state of mind, nothing is easier to miss than a Rall. or a cut. If you can combine the capacity of Desperate Dan with the reliability of Superman, good luck – but otherwise know where your limits are.

If you are away you will be expected to find your own accommodation. This can be a problem in certain places, particularly if there is a big festival on. Try to get to your destination early if you have not already booked. The theatre noticeboard is sometimes a good source of reasonable 'digs', but remember that the good ones are usually taken early. If you have a few days' notice, phone up the theatre and ask them to send you their own list if they have one. The local tourist board can be helpful or one of the national holiday bed and breakfast guides.

WEST END SHOWS

These often form a large part of freelancers' work and can provide, (at least as long as the show runs), a regular guaranteed income. Most shows when they have been running for a while, allow their players a fair and flexible system for taking time off. This allows them to avoid the mental and physical damage which could result from playing the same piece day after day. Almost all shows require that you agree to an exclusive period when you must attend every call and deputies are strictly not allowed. The length of this period varies but generally it is between one month and six weeks. Most players find this frustrating as they frequently have to turn down more attractive or lucrative work. The long term benefits, particularly if it is a successful show will usually outweigh these disadvantages. Although there are not benefits such as sick pay, the S.W.E.T. (Society of West End Theatres) employers will pay national insurance contributions on your behalf if you wish them to, and you will be eligible for holiday pay of one full weeks money for every three months of employment

When you work in the West End it may be the first time that you play with particular kinds and combinations of instruments – for example, drum kits and synthesizers. It might also be the first time that you have played with jazz musicians – unless of course you studied jazz at college. One comforting thing is that you will almost never be asked to improvise over a chord sequence; that still remains the province of the trained jazz musician. You do however have to learn to interpret the 'feel' of a new style of playing. Some arrangers attempt to communicate the style in which they want the piece played, by writing the jazz or swing rhythms without using conventional notation. In these cases they usually write 'swing' or some similar indication above the passage, so you should know the differences between the various styles. If you are in any doubt, listen to the players around you and fit in with the way that they are playing. In these kind of arrangements, the expression markings are played in a more exaggerated fashion than in standard classical music. Phrasing is on the whole more important in this kind of music and must be followed exactly if you are not to upset the ensemble.

I am always amazed at the thorough grasp of harmony demonstrated by most jazz musicians. As improvisation involves literally spontaneous composition, their knowledge allows them to become totally immersed in their performance. Classical musicians often find great difficulties when they have to improvise – as is sometimes necessary in avant-garde music. Even without a real knowledge of the disciplines involved in improvisation, just 'messing around' on the instrument, from time to time, can help break down barriers that exist between instrument and player after years of concentrating solely on the technical difficulties of one's individual part, rather than exploring the music that can be produced just for its own sake.

The rehearsal period of a new show can be exciting, as you are part of a creative process. It can also be frustrating as you wrestle with copying mistakes, re-writes, edits and a host of other changes. Always mark your parts clearly at rehearsals in a light pencil to begin with. You may end up rubbing them out several times. It is essential to mark them legibly, as almost certainly you will have to communicate to someone who has never seen the show before, exactly how it is to be played. Keeping deps. in the picture not only makes their job easier but it helps prevent their making very obvious mistakes, which would make it difficult for you next time you ask for time off.

DEPPING' IN THE WEST END

As a dep. in a show, you will normally 'sit in' for one or two performances. You almost certainly will not be able to see what is happening on stage and will be cramped and uncomfortable as you try to make sense of the horn part as it is flashing past. Take a pen and paper in with you and jot down the numbers that seem to present difficulties, in order to have another look at them before your first performance. Some shows have a duplicate copy of the part, which you can follow and then take home to practise. This is by far the best way to prepare yourself. On your debut, introduce yourself to the players around you and tell them – if they don't already know – that it is your first time. If they are not first time deps. themselves, they might be able to help you. If there are other horns in the show they'll be keeping an eye on you as well but don't rely on it. If they know the part well and engage 'automatic pilot', they might just forget that you are there. Also if you can, reintroduce yourself to the musical director; who might be just as switched off as anybody else and who might take a while to notice that there is a new face in the pit. The odd nod and lead works wonders and can sometimes shift some of the burden from your shoulders. If something does go amiss you might get "I'm sorry, wasn't I very clear?", even though you were ten bars adrift at the time!

Most theatres have a sophisticated sound system and it can be off-putting to try and equate what you are hearing in the pit with the noise that is booming around the theatre. You cannot always allow for the resident sound engineer to cater for the fact that you sit further from the mike or play more forcefully than the usual player. Follow the dynamics and USE YOUR EARS. Use your eyes too; if the M.D. appears to be trying to swat a fly while looking in your direction, play a little quieter!

The process of actually becoming known to West End fixers and players is, on the face of it, more difficult than making yourself known on the classical circuit. While it is possible to phone the busier fixers and send them a C.V. they rarely if ever audition players and will just refer your letter to the regular player, who will probably only make a note of your number to use in case of emergencies. It might be more effective to find out which players do which shows and write them a letter tactfully introducing yourself. If they like the tone of your letter they might find out more about you, (the grapevine is more efficient than you would think). As the whole scene has a high social factor, a chance meeting in a pub can often do just as well as the most eloquent letter. I am not suggesting that you hang around West End pubs pestering tired horn players, but if you do happen to be introduced, enjoy the general atmosphere and a drink or two and if you leave behind a good impression you might be asked to come and sit in.

Playing in a pit, however good, presents problems. You might find that you are a long way from the sections of the orchestra that you are supposed to be playing with and you cannot really hear them. This can result in problems with both intonation and ensemble. The ensemble problem can be helped by following the conductor's beat as closely as you can, regardless of what you are hearing. Often the rest of the brass will be on the other side of the pit and you will hear them fractionally late. This can be off-putting, particularly if you are sight reading. Regarding intonation, if you are playing in a section, follow the intonation of the first horn. If you are principal, listen carefully to the tuning 'A' and stay as faithful to that as you can.

An additional problem in West End pits, is that they are usually very small and cramped. Due to the understandable fact that no-one wants to sit behind the horn players, you will more often than not find yourself playing directly into a wall. This has the effect of making you appear sharp in relation to the rest of the band. This is difficult to deal with and my only advice is just to be aware of this fact and provided that the band isn't playing at a radically different pitch from the one that you are used to, just place the notes where you normally would and try to disregard the apparent difference. Some of these shows even though they do not look much of a blow on paper, actually turn out to be quite tiring. As for ballet, pace yourself carefully – even though you might just get through the second show without 'blowing up', you will probably damage your lip and of course, there's always tomorrow to think of.....

LIP FIRST AID

On the subject of lip first-aid, if you feel that you have bruised or damaged your lip, just running an ice cube over them for a few minutes last thing at night, can reduce any swelling and in the morning they can be revitalised by putting alternate hot and cold flannels on them for a few minutes. This helps to stimulate the muscles and the blood vessels, but be sure that you finish off with a cold one. For the homeopathically inclined, 'Arnica', in tablet form, works very well; particularly in a preventative capacity when you know that you have a lot of blowing to do. Taken morning and night it seems to help the muscles keep in good shape.

Finally, 'depping' in a show means that you are looking after someone else's job. They have entrusted you with something important to them, so do all that you can to make the show go unobtrusively smoothly. The other members of the band will be certain to pass on their impressions to the regular player. You have to make sure that they are favourable ones.

LOOKING AFTER YOUR DIARY

One of the most frustrating aspects of freelancing is when having taken on one date, a more interesting or lucrative one is offered to you. Generally speaking, most fixers are flexible and given adequate notice will try to be sympathetic. However, when you are trying to establish yourself as a freelance player you must tread very carefully. In favour of trying to substitute a date might be:

1. That it is a new and potentially useful contact.
2. That it is a more prestigious date.
3. It is better paid.
4. More musically satisfying.
5. More fun!

Against these you must consider that you are a new quantity to a fixer, who will probably think that he/she is helping you by offering the work in the first place. The last thing that you want to do is get a reputation for being unreliable. Finding a replacement for you will involve extra work for the already busy fixer. Although you could offer to do this, most fixers will prefer to do it for themselves. A polite and regretful refusal will not exclude you from the possibility of being offered future dates, but a bad reputation will travel fast and far. Just ask yourself this question – if you were a fixer how would <u>you</u> feel about granting your request? Would you think that it was fair, or would you think that you were more trouble than you were worth? If you still think that it is worthwhile, go ahead and ask, but do it tactfully and carefully. If you say something like "I'm sorry to trouble you, but I have the offer of a date which I would very much like to accept, only it clashes with the date that you have offered me on ...." and explain why you particularly want to do the other date – obviously avoiding such reasons as: "It's more money" or "It's more fun". Fixers have a very good idea of how much each date is worth, so just telling them what you are doing is enough. Ask them how they would feel about releasing you and listen carefully to their first reaction. If they start to explain that it is a busy day, and that it would be difficult to find a replacement, it probably means that they tried a lot of other players before they got to you. You could offer to help them by suggesting other players, but if they haven't already tried them, they probably don't know them and they would not be keen on taking a chance. If you press your case further you risk losing that contact.

You may feel sometimes that a fixer is being unfair to you, but remember, however modest the organisation for whom they fix, at the moment you need them far more than they need you. You have to take personalities into account too – if a fixer has taken a liking to you as well as to your playing, he/she will be more willing to help you out. You will find that some fixers are unscrupulous, some even bordering on the dishonest. Some prefer to use younger players as they are more available and easier to manipulate. Sadly, in a profession which is becoming more competitive as the number of jobs diminishes, you will sometimes have to work with and for people whom you may not really like. Happily, though, most of the people you encounter will help you if they feel that you deserve it. You can never be right all the time, just keep your ears open, trust your own intuition and remember that as with any job, a friendly and frank relationship with your employer is the best for both sides.

DIARY SERVICES

Over the last twenty or so years the diary service has played an increasingly important part in the life of a freelance musician. The diary service holds copies of your diary, and dealing directly with the contractor, accepts engagements on your behalf. The advantage of this system is that at any time a fixer can check your availability, and book you no matter where you are. This can save them making many separate calls. Also if the particular player that they want is not free, they can ask the service to suggest an alternative. This can be advantageous to you, as you may get a date from a new fixer who is prepared to take a chance on an unknown quantity. Once a diary service gets to know you, although they are not usually in the business of actively trying to promote their clients, they could give the fixer a brief description of the kind of work you do, and this might be enough to prompt him or her to try you.

The larger diary services do not offer to get you work. Some will not put you on their books if you do not already have a few established contacts. This could be frustrating, but it is also very fair: it would be too easy to take your money and do nothing in return. Some services do promise to help you find contacts, but you should not rely on this too much. The music business is like many others, in a recession, and it is unlikely that these services would be able to find you a substantial amount of work that you would not otherwise have been offered. The fees are generally around a session fee (£80.00) a quarter. If you do join a diary service and find that you are not getting any benefit from it, there is nothing to stop you from leaving and re-joining at a time when it may be of more use to you.

RADIO PAGING

Many diary services now offer a radio-paging service. Briefly, this means that they will page you when there is any work to collect, or if someone wishes to contact you urgently about a date. Radio-paging is not particularly cheap and must earn its keep. Any bonus points you may think result from just having a pager are quickly lost if it's never seen to go off! To a certain extent, when you join a diary service, some of the control which you have over your bookings is removed. A diary service is only as helpful as the information that you give them, about exactly what you want them to do on your behalf. An experienced diary service will refer clashes of work if they feel that you might prefer taking the latest date. They will, if you wish, refer every new offer of work and leave you to decide – although this can be unhelpful to a fixer if a quick answer is wanted. Inevitably the service will sometimes make a mistake, but if you build up a good relationship with them they can be an enormous help to you.

One alternative to a diary service is having someone at home more or less permanently to answer the phone and take bookings. If you still live at home, a member of your family is the cheapest. Even if you no longer live at home, you could use that number for your business calls. The obvious drawback is that your relations cannot stay at home all the time just for your benefit; also many fixers will prefer to deal directly with you. An answering machine is invaluable, particularly one with a remote controller. It is important that if you leave a message to say "I'll get back to you shortly", you are able to do so wherever you are. It is a bit demoralising to phone in three times a day only to find that there are no messages; but if a fixer does leave a message, your prompt reply might persuade him/her to use you again.

In the early days of freelancing, West End shows might be a large part of your work, and this is where a diary service can be very useful. Most of your dates will probably be at short notice – perhaps the usual player is too tired to do the evening show – and if you are free they will want to know immediately if you will dep. If you were out of the house, you could miss the call, and then they would move on to someone else. Even if you have an answering machine, it cannot give the positive answer that is wanted. On the other hand, the diary service, especially if you have a pager, will guarantee that you get the date, or at least will give you the best chance of not missing out.

THE MUSICIAN'S UNION

Since legislation was passed making 'closed shop' unions illegal, it is no longer necessary to be a member of the Musician's Union to operate as a professional musician. Not surprisingly though, very few musicians have decided to leave the union. One reason for this may be the important contribution to our lives, that the Union makes. In recent years the Union has come in for a great deal of criticism over the way in which it represents our interests. Some of this criticism is probably quite valid; but this must not be allowed to overshadow the enormous amount of good work that it does on our behalf. I mention this because I have noticed, particularly among some of the younger players, a feeling of "why do we need the Union at all?"

During the 1960's and 1970's, before the recession began to take effect, the musical scene in London was thriving. The top players had more work than they could handle. As a result of this, all players, of all abilities were able to earn a comfortable living. Due partly to lack of interest, and partly simply being too busy, many player's involvement with the Union dwindled to just paying their subscriptions, and attendance at Union meetings declined. As policies and rates are decided at these meetings, Union officials found that they were having to make important decisions without as much 'feedback' from the membership as they would have liked. Over the years, this has led to them being criticised for not reflecting the interests and needs of their professional members.

I think it is important to be aware that if you criticise the Union, you are in fact criticising yourself. YOU are the Union, and it can never function efficiently without the full support and commitment of its membership. Many of the people who are outspoken critics of the Union in the tea-break, have never made the effort to attend a meeting, and in some cases don't even bother to return postal ballot forms!

The Union does far more than just negotiate fees. It is largely responsible for the creation of our working conditions. Our beloved tea-breaks are of a reasonable length, not by divine right, but as a result of negotiations between the Union and our employers. There will always be both unscrupulous employers, and honest ones; having an agreement negotiated by the Union, on our behalf, ensures that we can get on with doing what we do best – making music – without having to worry too much about getting ripped off.

No matter how careful you are, sooner or later it is likely that a problem will arise between you, and an employer. In these situations, you will often find you are on your own. For one reason or another, most musicians are reluctant to 'stick their heads above the parapet' as it were. By that I mean to speak out for or against something, when it might bring them into conflict with their employers – even if it is on their own behalf. People can be very positive and outspoken in the tea-break, or the pub, but you will often find such support melts away when they are actually required to do something. At times like these the Union can be your best friend, and can represent your interests fairly and reliably; provided of course that you in turn support their efforts.

I have set out here a few of the reasons why I think the Union is 'good news' for musicians; you must make up your own mind. Whatever you personally decide, without doubt the future of the Musicians' Union as a body able to effectively represent the interests of professional musicians, lies in the hands of the next generation of players. Without their support I think it unlikely that we shall be able to enjoy the benefits of our Union very far into the next century.

WORKING WITH THE PRINCIPAL ORCHESTRAS

When you walk into your first rehearsal with one of the main orchestras you will probably get the feeling that you are entering a party where everybody knows one another except you. Snatches of discussions about the last tour, in-jokes and even simple things such as wondering where the toilets are, increase the impression that you are an outsider. After taking all this in, you have then got to take out your instrument and play your best, probably in a piece that is unfamiliar to you. It's a lot to cope with at once but you can take a little comfort from the knowledge that everyone in the room has had to undergo the same experience at one time or another.

If you have decided that you want to spend your playing life as a member of a symphony or chamber orchestra, then you will probably not have to repeat this experience too many times. If, however, you decide to remain freelance, you will have to repeat this scenario many times before you have 'covered all the ground', so to speak. It does get easier though, as there will be other players 'doing the rounds' and as time goes by you will find an increasing number of friendly faces to talk to.

Horn players are generally a kind and helpful breed, but as there is a special bond that develops in an established section that is the natural result of spending a lot of time playing and travelling together, this will at first increase your feeling of 'outsiderness'. Jeffrey Bryant gives you some solid gold rules about how to approach the job of fitting in successfully as a 'new boy', but it will always take time until you start to feel a little more at home.

One of the things that will probably impress you most is just how GOOD the other players are. This can either sap your confidence or inspire you to play better than you ever thought that you could.

Probably, you will end up with a mixture of both for a while. Remember, though, that as in any job, the players rely on 'tricks of the trade' which no amount of practising at home can teach you, to get round awkward moments which you will go to meet 'head on'. The point that I want to make is that these are natural and inevitable parts of the job that you have chosen to learn, so you need not feel too overwhelmed by what you see and hear around you.

ORCHESTRAL POLITICS

Let's assume that you have played well enough to be asked to come into the orchestra on a regular basis and you are starting to make friends with the rest of the section. As their confidence in you grows, you may find that you are introduced to a new aspect of freelance work, POLITICS. It is important to avoid becoming too involved. In any family there are undercurrents, little alliances, conflicts and intrigues. In the 'hothouse atmosphere' of the orchestra, charged as it is with emotion and stress, they are a fact of life. All orchestras are affected to a greater or lesser degree. A player who is a full time member of an orchestra rarely gets the chance to see players from other orchestras, so you, as an extra hopefully working with as many of them as possible, can be a welcome source of news; this is particularly true if you are working with orchestras in another part of the country. This part of your job will sooner or later prompt people to take you into their confidence with their own POLITICAL problems. This is natural, as you can provide a neutral opinion if you are asked for one. However, tread very carefully here, particularly if it involves problems within the section. You may find that you are expected to sympathise with opposing sides of a situation that you, as an outsider, can never fully comprehend. Because of the nature of the job, musicians – and horn players in particular – can have their confidence easily undermined and so it is vital for survival that he, or she finds an inner strength to sustain them when things are not going well. Even so, if another established player is kind enough to take you into his/her confidence, remember two things: first of all, as cynical as it may sound, there is rarely such a thing as complete confidentiality. Secondly, as often happens when someone shares a problem, it is the act of telling another person that is important, not necessarily the answer received. You, as a newcomer, are not able to offer informed advice. That is as good a reason as any for excusing yourself from commenting. Your honesty and humility will eventually be appreciated.

CONCERT TECHNIQUE

Much of your work with the large orchestras will be as an additional horn in one of the large scale works. You will certainly get to know Mahler and Bruckner fairly well and have more than a passing acquaintance with Richard Strauss. This usually means that you will only be involved in one part of the programme. The problem here, is that you are sitting down to play a difficult piece in a section that has already had time to get settled in to the concert. You can help yourself by arriving early enough to have a blow, then go and have a cup of tea or something, then have another little blow. Do this a few times until you feel more relaxed, then leave it until you go on stage. Even then, just hang back on the dynamics a little until you feel confident.

Nobody plays well all the time and in the early days you will more than once come away wishing that you had stayed at home. The temptation here is to feel that you need to apologise to someone. There are always excuses to be found, many are reasonable and quite valid, but the truth is that no-one really wants to hear them. For the section, it's another concert over, and time maybe for a pint or two and a chat in the pub; they are not going to want to listen to your problems. If you must say something, wrap it up in a constructive comment such as 'This horn section plays so strongly I found it a bit hard to keep up.' You see, they will probably have made their own assessment of what your strengths and weaknesses are, and while they will privately sympathise with you, they know that the only way to progress is to put bad concerts behind you, analyse what went wrong and practise to put it right. If they feel that you have the right qualities in you, you will get another chance.

Some lucky players seem to have an 'old head on young shoulders' and can adapt to any new situation without letting nerves affect their performance. If you don't happen to be one of these don't worry, they are in the minority and the rest of us seem to get there in the end. All through your playing career you will come across players who are greater than, or not as able as, yourself. There is much to be learned from both kinds if you can avoid the trap of allowing yourself to feel either inadequate, or superior in relation to them. If you feel that you have played badly on a date, talk it over with your professor and without doubt something good will come out of the experience.

THE BAD TIMES

Freelancing is hard. Sometimes very hard; you will have to learn to be your own life support system. Apart from the day-to-day business of organising your diary and getting to work, you will have to look after all the physical and psychological aspects of operating a one person hornplaying business. The diverse kinds of playing, and circumstances under which you are required to perform, take their toll on both your lip, and your sanity. From time to time this can lead to serious technical problems; make no mistake, there are few more daunting tasks than having to carry on turning out a good 'product' so to speak, when everything that you thought that you had under control about your playing has deserted you.

These things happen, at some time or another, to everyone. There is a great deal that you can do to help yourself through these sometimes privately desperate times. The first thing to do, is follow the advice of the 'Hitchiker's Guide to the Galaxy' - don't panic! Most problems start out as slight physical changes which interfere with ones' natural playing style. Unless you are able to isolate what has gone wrong and make the usually minor adjustments to rectify it, the next step is often increased pressure and tension in the arms and upper body, which might get you through a couple more shows before things _really_ start to pack up on you.

If this does happen, before you throw your instrument under the nearest bus, sit down quietly, on your own, and <u>think</u>. If your lips have become swollen – blowing too much, or even at the change of seasons, going from warm to cold and windy weather can be the cause – you will have to compensate for this until the swelling subsides. Just 'back off' notes a bit and try and buzz them rather more than you normally do, and that should help. Tiredness and tension often go hand in hand; they are among the arch-enemies of all players. 'Sod's Law' seems to be quite active in the freelance profession. Very often the negative factors appear to converge on precisely the day that you are working for a new 'fixer', or have a difficult piece to play. These factors are often self generating. If you can find no <u>honest</u> physical reasons why you should suddenly be splitting middle 'C' with agonizing frequency, then you are probably conjuring up your own mental demons, something which horn players are particularly good at. If I suggest to you that the thing to do is relax and unwind yourself a couple of turns, it will probably seem about as much use as your dentist telling you that if you relax when he sticks a needle into your gums, it won't hurt!

The parallel here is that you know from experience that needles are painful, just as you have learned that stress and tension can make you play badly. To be fair to dentists, if you are able to relax of course, it is less painful, and you can apply the same techniques to playing. Things do not have to remain a problem just because they always have been, but it takes time, Each crisis that you deal with in a positive way, will allow you to deal more efficiently with the next.

Things can get absurdly out of proportion when the nerves start to assert themselves. It is easy to imagine being nervous at the prospect of playing a difficult concerto in front of a few thousand people, but what kind of sense does it make to worry almost as much about, for example, playing a middle register note for a couple of bars, just because if happens to be solo?

As laughable as it may sound, in your early days of freelancing, this is the kind of thing that can cause problems if you are going through a bad patch. The remedy is the same every time; back off, get the problem in perspective, and don't let the demons get the upper hand. The imagination which might enable you to play a phrase in a fresh and original way, can also be responsible for making life more difficult. Once when I was working with an orchestra with whom I was anxious to make a good impression, I 'knocked over' more notes than I wanted to. After the concert when we were changing in the dressing room, I became convinced that nobody was talking to me as a result of my duff performance. I went home in a very depressed state. The next night we repeated the concert and fortunately, everything went well but – yes, you guessed it, nobody said a word to me afterwards! Musicians live in their own private worlds most of the time so don't let your imagination weave meaning into innocent situations.

One of the unfortunate paradoxes of this business is that, the more successful you are, the busier and therefore more tired and prone to the musician's own special brand of problems. Therefore, as difficult and unimportant as it may seem at the time, when you (hopefully) do start to become busy, make sure that rest and regular exercise don't get pushed off of the schedule.

Each challenge that you face, and overcome, will make you a more complete player. Even the ones that get the better of you are not necessarily complete failures, as long as you learn from them and remember – as trite as it may sound – that there is much, much more to life than that ridiculous brass pipe.

STAGE PRESENCE

Although the sea of faces that hopefully are going to be waiting for you when you walk out on to the concert platform, are definitely not going to be looking at you all the time, it would be inappropriate to wander on the stage, slump in your seat, and with legs crossed, embark upon excerpts from the concerto repertoire until the whole orchestra assembled.   A concert is to some extent a ritual, in which both musicians, and audience participate; the sight of an orchestra in full evening dress, (well, that's what it looks like from a distance) is an integral part of the experience. At the end of the piece, to see them stand and bow together to acknowledge the applause, is a much more impressive sight than having them lumbering hesitantly to their feet a few at a time, grinning sheepishly at the audience, or even worse, fixing them with a stony stare that seems oblivious to their presence. The general rule is to watch the leader of the orchestra and stand up when he does; at the same time, be aware of the other members of the orchestra and stand up with the majority.

If you have played a solo and the conductor gestures you to stand up on your own, do so quickly and give a small bow to the audience and <u>smile</u> if you can. Sometimes you can get a bow even when you think that you have not played particularly well. It is times like these when you must behave as though you had turned in your best performance. This is because if there were any small slips, the audience will have noticed them a lot less than you and your composure might just persuade them that they did not hear any mistakes at all.

Personally, if I am playing 'down the line' I try not to stand up before the principals. They, after all, are the leaders, and I feel that it is a courtesy to them. Beware also of knocking over music stands as you get up, particularly if the platform is small; apart from being embarrassing, they can do a lot of damage as they fall.

When you are playing in a piece that has TACET movements for you, (for example the extra horns in Mahler Symphony No. 3), you will have to sit quietly for quite long periods of time. Put your horn on the floor if you can, somewhere where you wont kick it and try to get yourself comfortable. A lot of orchestras don't like you crossing your legs or slumping in your seat, so don't get too comfortable. Some words of warning about long pieces: know your bladder! It's bad enough wanting to 'go' when you have playing to distract you, but if you are just sitting there thinking about it, it can be murder. Some of it is psychological – you want to because you know you can't, – so unless you've drunk a lot of beer, you'll make the end of the concert without too much trouble.

One final story concerns a well-known player, who in his younger days was playing the third horn in the Saint-Saens Organ Symphony. In this piece, the third horn has most of the important solos and he had been practising hard for some weeks, in order to make a good impression on the section. He played his part beautifully, and as the conductor left the platform, he basked in the congratulations of his colleagues. As he sat enjoying the feeling of a job well done, the conductor returned to the platform and gestured in his direction. Flushed with success, he immediately sprang to his feet. Unfortunately for him, he had forgotten that in the Royal Festival Hall, the horns are often seated in front of the organ, and he found himself in the embarrassing situation of standing in front of an increasingly indignant organ soloist who was attempting to take his own bow. These things take a lot of living down!

TOURING WITH AN ORCHESTRA

Going on a tour, particularly a foreign one, can be incredible fun. Most of you will have done some kind of a tour during your studies, so you will probably have a rough idea of what to expect. However, on your first professional tour, there will be some considerable differences. First you will be getting paid and put up in usually quite good hotels, the subsistence will be perhaps more than you have had before and you will be going to new and far away places. Sounds like a good holiday doesn't it? The trouble is that you have to work, sometimes even harder than when you are home. Most people let their hair down a bit under these circumstances, but don't forget that the regular members have done this all before and know how to cope with the exertions of travelling and playing under unfamiliar conditions. There will be a touring manager alongside the normal orchestral 'fixer', and they will have a generally arduous time making sure that all the required players are present on stage in whatever town, at whatever time, and for whatever piece they are needed. What they do not need, is for a new face to give them any trouble. This means being on time for flights and coaches, having the correct dress, <u>not</u> locking your passport in your suitcase which has already been loaded onto the plane, or getting arrested. Touring can play havoc with your lip, so make sure that you are able to warm-up and practise every day that you can.

Often, your horn will be taken for you on the orchestral van. If the orchestra are doing several different programmes on the tour, you might find that you have one or more days off. If your horn is on the van, find the time to go into the hall and have a blow, it'll make you feel better and will help keep your chops in order. Going away on tour will really give you the feel of what it's like to be in the orchestra, and playing with the section regularly over a period of maybe several weeks, can do your playing a lot of good. Just a word of warning though – no-one can really play their best with a dreadful hangover. You still have to do the job that you are being paid for. Just feel your way carefully until you know what you can and can't cope with, and you can still have a good time into the bargain.

PROVINCIAL ORCHESTRAS

The provincial orchestras have much to offer the freelance player. Whether it is to fill in when they have a vacant position, or to provide extra players for large scale works, they have a healthy amount of employment available. The great advantage of working with these orchestras, lies firstly in the way that their schedule provides for repeat concerts of the same programme over each week. This means that you can really get to know each piece and try to improve your performance each time. The atmosphere is more relaxed than in London, and very often the average age of the section is much younger. This is more fun generally, but it also means that you get to hear at first hand, the people of your generation – or slightly older, who have 'made it' – and you can get an idea of the standards which you must aspire to if you wish to follow in their footsteps.

There is almost always a good social scene in these orchestras, and provided you recognise that as in other full-time groups, they are a self-contained and close-knit community with a consciousness of, and pride in their own identity, and you don't go in with a 'Hey, look-at-me' attitude, you will find that you will quickly be admitted into the 'family' and will learn many valuable lessons. As Frank Lloyd has already talked about the overall standards that prevail in these orchestras, I will only add that your first rehearsal with a provincial orchestra can leave you feeling just as lost and inadequate, as your first taste of the London bands. The difference is that there is more time allowed for rehearsal, and therefore more chance for you to get to know your part, practise it, and settle-in to the section. The odd mistake won't seem as disastrous as it might under other circumstances, but on the show you will still be expected to perform to your highest possible standard.

THE WAGNER TUBA

You will probably be asked to play the Wagner tuba at some time. Hopefully you will have had a chance to get to know these instruments while you are at college. It is well worth learning the most famous pieces in the tuba repertoire on all parts. Those which seem to come around more than others are the Bruckner symphonies Nos. 7,8,9, the 'Rite of Spring', and the orchestral excerpts from the 'Ring' cycle. More often than not, if you do not own an instrument of your own, you will have only a few minutes to get to know the tuba that you are going to have to play. The quality of these instruments varies from set to set, and while some of them are quite good, as a new boy you might find yourself with the 'runt of the litter', so to speak. This is when having become familiar with the parts will pay dividends. You want to be able to concentrate solely on making the reluctant instrument play the notes that you require in tune, rather than struggling with the sometimes unnecessarily awkward transpositions.

If the tuba quartet gets a chance to blow a few notes and tune together before the rehearsal, then that will help enormously. Otherwise, think hard about the pitch and 'make' the note yourself without any help from the instrument, by using lots of diaphragm support and plenty of air to fill the tuba and make a good sound. You will usually get an extra fee for playing the tuba. On the whole you will certainly earn it, but I always find that on the occasions when everything seems to work for a tuba quartet, it is one of the best parts of the job.

THE RIGHT PLACE, THE RIGHT DRESS

There are a few things to mention about the general business of freelancing. The first is about bringing the right dress with you. This may seem straightforward enough, but once your diary becomes a mixture of different kinds of work, it is surprising how many times you can get caught out. Tails are the normal dress for symphony orchestras of course, although sometimes during the summer, particularly for a 'pops' concert, a white jacket is required. Dinner jackets are generally needed for Opera and Ballet and occasionally for choral dates with large orchestras. A West End show will be either dinner jacket, or black shirt and trousers. For the ladies it is not quite so straightforward, the usual alternatives of long black, long coloured, short black etc. will vary from date to date.

A checking routine is valuable before you leave the house. I use this one:

1. Check the diary to reassure yourself of the date, time and the venue. If it is somewhere that you have never been before, look it up on the map or A–Z. If it looks tricky, then bring the A–Z with you.
2. Check the dress, if there is no mention of it in the diary, then call the fixer or the orchestral office. If you get no reply, try phoning someone whom you think might be on the date. If you still cannot find out what it is, you'll have to bring the lot. You'll be carrying a heavy bag and probably cursing when you get there, but it will save you any potential embarrassment.
3. Check what you have put in your gig bag. Make sure that you have all the clothes (including black socks, bow ties and cuff links) and music, schedules, addresses etc. that you need. Just as you close your front door, mentally check them again – it's worth it!

TAX AND VAT

One thing I really would recommend is to put money aside from your first regular engagements for your future tax liability. I speak from bitter experience. I know that with all the things that you will want to do with your money – cars, houses, curries etc – this might assume quite a low priority. Sooner or later though, you will have to pay both tax and national insurance, and your first bill will cover your years at college too! It is a good idea to talk to an accountant as well, particularly one whom you know has other musicians on his/her books. Fees are not cheap, but an accountant will help you by ensuring that you claim for all the allowances which can be offset against your tax liability, and that usually means that you save much more than you payout. Later on be aware of the limit beyond which you will have to register for VAT. It can be a very expensive omission. If VAT officers believe that you should have been registered for VAT over a certain period and you were not, they will charge you the tax which you will have to pay immediately, plus a fine. It will be up to you then to try and recover some, or all of the tax by writing to every single employer that you had, for every date during the period in question. As you can see, that situation is best avoided. The present VAT threshold is £36,000 which gives most of us plenty of headroom. Remember though that this is turnover and not profit.

PENSIONS AND HEALTH INSURANCE

Also on the subject of money, we have to provide for our own pension and the sooner we get started the better. Even just a small standing order each month can get you off to a good start, and it will give you a good feeling later on to know that the day will come when you can afford to hang up your horn if you want to. There are many companies offering a wide variety of schemes; ideally you want one that will allow you to suspend contributions if times get hard, and also maybe pay in the odd lump sum when you have some spare cash. Later on, especially if you have taken on commitments such as a huge mortgage, you might consider some form of health insurance. Here there are fewer options open to us. You have to be careful when you take out the policy, that it will pay you if you are not able to pursue your <u>normal</u> occupation. This is important, particularly as an injury to the teeth might not be considered as an incapacitating one. Generally speaking, accident insurance is cheaper than so called 'permanent health' insurance, which covers illness as well. Read the small print carefully, as most only pay for a specified length of time before the benefits are either reviewed, or curtailed. There are also a few 'friendly benefit societies' within the profession which you might join. These will pay out a modest amount each week to a member who is unable to work, with the cost being shared equally among the other working members. These are cost effective, as you only have to pay out when someone is actually incapacitated, and the amount is usually very small.

There is a surprising amount of paperwork attached to being a professional musician, and all of us agree that it is one of the dullest parts of the job. It is very easy to push it in a corner and forget about it, especially if you are working hard at the time. If you can, just deal with it as it arrives and you will find the task less daunting. This is particularly true when it comes to your accounts. Get a book and note down what you have been paid and by whom. If you buy an account book, you can put down your relevant expenses as well. This will save you a lot of time when you come to prepare your tax.

CODA

As I mentioned earlier, excellent sight-reading is essential to be a useful freelancer; as is the ability to play both high and low horn, Wagner tuba and be in two places at once. Concerning the best kind of instrument, while an F alto is favoured by many players, I think that it is nice to have one in reserve but a good double or single that has a useful F extension will do for most situations. A good pair of ears will be your best friends, as you are going to have to fit in, chameleon-like, with all the players' sections that employ you, and yet still retain the essential character of your own playing.

Taking care of yourself physically is vital, as you will be working long hours and need to function at your best even after a long day of continuous concentration. Exercise helps you unwind both mentally and physically; you will be able to cope with much more in terms of stress if you feel good. It can be difficult to fit it in on a regular basis, but will pay dividends, even if you do just a little when you can. For instance walking, if you have the time, rather than taking the tube or bus, will relax you and keep you healthy.

Finally, I would just give one really essential piece of advice: <u>stick at it</u>, it's the only way. You will get times when you will want to scream with frustration, times of despair when just nothing seems to be going right, times when your diary looks as white as a ski slope and you doubt that anyone will ever book you again. They <u>will</u> book you if you are honest about your own strengths and weaknesses and are reliable and easy to get on with. One of the reasons why I felt that I was qualified to attempt to write this chapter, was that I have made every mistake in the book at least twice, but I am still enjoying being a freelance horn player and am still <u>learning</u> about the business. I think that may be the key – learn from your mistakes and if people see that, then they will more than likely give you as many chances as you deserve.

INDEX

A
Alcohol	15, 77, 94
Accommodation	94
Answering Machines	53, 101
Auditions	32
Auditions: Music for ballet	36
Auditions: Music for opera	37
Attitude	61, 112
Agents	80

B
Ballet	36, 93
Bumping up	8
Brass Quintet	73

C
Confidence	9, 32
Concert technique	16, 106
Concentration	26, 44, 79
Click track	47
Conductors	24, 96
Chamber music	62, 65
Cold Churches, playing in	70
Contacts, making	62, 97
Choreography in brass quintet performance	73
Character	5, 61, 107

D
Deputising in West End	96
Diaphragm	93, 113
Diary: Management of	98, 101
Services	53, 100
Dress	114
Dynamics	7, 24, 35, 66, 67

E
Ensemble Playing ... 66, 72
Excuses ... 74, 106
Excerpts, performance of ... 32

F
Freelancing: Coping with ... 92, 107
             General ... 90
Film sessions ... 49
First horn, playing ... 13
Financial aspects ... 30
Fixers (contractors) ... 4, 52, 97, 99, 100
Fourth Horn Playing ... 12

G
Getting onto
  orchestral managers' lists: ... 62, 63, 92, 97

H
Harmonics ... 68, 75
Handstopping ... 33, 48

I
Insurance ... 115
Instrument – choice of ... 6, 50, 64, 116
Intonation ... 11, 23, 47, 68, 69, 70, 97

J
James Brown ... 47
Jazz phrasing ... 46, 95

K
Keeping fit ... 79, 117

L
Lips: Preparation of ... 16, 42, 79
       First Aid of ... 98
       Strengthening of ... 42, 79

M
Making the most of opportunities	5
Memory, performing from	
Musician's Union	102

N
Nerves, control of	51, 77, 78, 108

O
Opera		22, 45
Orchestras:	Working with principal	104
	Chamber	
	Provincial	82, 112
Organising yourself		53, 114

P
Pits, orchestral	23, 97
Politics	90, 105
Pensions	30, 115
Practise	42, 51, 74, 75
Playing standards	59
Pitch, problems with	70
Presentation	73
Psychological aspects of playing	107

Q
Quiet playing	7, 13, 67

R
Radio paging	101
Running your own group	72
Repertoire	36, 37, 38, 84
Recital, planning a	81

S

Second horn playing	10, 63
Section Playing	7, 45, 46
Fitting into	6
Solo performing	76, 78
Stage bands	26
Sight reading	92
Stage presence	109
Studios, names of main	50
Style	31, 45
Social behaviour	15, 61, 93, 104, 112
Sponsorship	72
Synthesizers	48
Stress	77, 108
Sound	34
Session work	52

T

Touring opera and ballet	91
Touring with orchestra	111
Tax and VAT	115
Third horn	11
Tuckwell, Barry	76

V

Vibrato	11, 47

W

West End shows	94
Wagner tuba	27, 113
Warm up	15, 44